T0140334

Socio-Affective Computing

Volume 10

Series Editors

Amir Hussain, University of Stirling, Stirling, UK

Erik Cambria, Nanyang Technological University, Singapore, Singapore

This exciting series publishes state-of-the-art research on socially intelligent, affective, and multimodal human-machine interaction and systems. It emphasizes the role of affect in social interactions and the humanistic side of affective computing by promoting publications at the crossroads between computer science, engineering and the human sciences (including biological, social, and cultural aspects of human life).

Three broad domains of social and affective computing will be covered by the book series: social computing; affective computing; and the interplay of these domains (for example, augmenting social interaction through affective computing).

Examples of the first domain include all types of social interactions that contribute to meaning, interest, and richness in our daily life, e.g., information produced by a group of people used to provide or enhance the functioning of a system. Examples of the second domain include computational and psychological models of emotions, bodily manifestations of affect (facial expressions, posture, behavior, physiology), and affective interfaces and applications, e.g., dialogue systems, games, and learning.

Research monographs, introductory- and advanced-level textbooks, and edited volumes are considered for the series.

More information about this series at http://www.springer.com/series/13199

Xiaoshi Zhong • Erik Cambria

Time Expression and Named Entity Recognition

Springer

Xiaoshi Zhong
Beijing Institute of Technology
School of Computer Science
and Technology
Beijing, China

Erik Cambria
Nanyang Technological University
School of Computer Science
and Engineering
Singapore, Singapore

ISSN 2509-5706   ISSN 2509-5714   (electronic)
Socio-Affective Computing
ISBN 978-3-030-78963-3   ISBN 978-3-030-78961-9   (eBook)
https://doi.org/10.1007/978-3-030-78961-9

This Springer imprint is published by the registered company Springer Nature Switzerland AG.
The registered company address is: Gewerbestrasse 11, 6330 Cham, Switzerland

Preface

Everything should be made as simple as possible, but not simpler.
–Albert Einstein

The content of this book is mainly derived from the thesis of my Doctor of Philosophy degree [2]. During my doctoral study in the School of Computer Science and Engineering at Nanyang Technological University, I was fortunate to conduct research under the supervision of Prof. Erik Cambria and Prof. Jagath C. Rajapakse. Besides being a nice supervisor, Erik is also a good friend and a great leader. Jagath is a nice professor who has tolerated my poor spoken English for 2 years. Without the support from Erik and Jagath, it would not have been possible for me to complete my dissertation.

To better illustrate my research results and how they come, I use the diagram shown in Fig. 1 to briefly introduce my research style. In most scientific research, the general paradigm is the "hypothesis + verification" procedure: for a problem, we first of all have a rough idea or guess or conjuncture about this problem, and then formulate this conjuncture into a hypothesis; after that, we collect numerous data or concrete evidence to verify whether the hypothesis is true or not. When we apply this paradigm to the research on the fields of data analytics, computational linguistics, natural language processing, and other data-science areas, there involve two important components: *data characteristics* and *model assumptions*.

In current natural language processing, many works mainly propose models and then use data to evaluate the quality of these models according to some criteria such as precision, recall, and F_1 score. Almost all these works however are explicitly or implicitly verifying whether the assumptions of proposed models fit the characteristics of data. Fig. 1, if model assumptions fit data characteristics, then proposed models will achieve good results; otherwise, we need to design a new model that fits the characteristics of analyzed data. The current research in natural language processing tends to concentrate more attention on proposing new models while ignoring to analyze data characteristics. My research style instead is to first analyze data characteristics and then design appropriate models according to these characteristics for specific tasks. Such a style can not only enhance my understanding into a task and data, but also enhance the probability that the

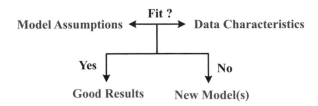

Fig. 1 Scientific paradigm "hypothesis + verification" in data analytics: examine whether model assumptions fit data characteristics. When model assumptions fit data characteristics, we will get good results, otherwise, we need to develop a new model so as to fit data characteristics

assumptions of my designed model fit data characteristics and therefore lead my model to achieve good results. Moreover, since I have a better understanding about model assumptions and data characteristics, I can also interpret these results and explain the advantage and disadvantage of my model.

In this book, I focus on analyzing common characteristics of time expressions and named entities from diverse datasets, and then according to these characteristics design effective and efficient algorithms for recognizing time expressions and named entities from unstructured text.

When analyzing time expressions, I believe that there must be some common characteristics in diverse datasets, because we humans share some common habits to express time information, no matter what platforms we are expressing on and no matter what topics we are talking about. In the moment when I figured out that there are only about 70 distinct time tokens in an individual dataset and only about 125 distinct time tokens across four diverse datasets, I knew that my conjecture is verified. Regarding why I define token types that separate rules and specific tokens, and then design general heuristic rules that works on token types and that are independent of specific tokens, at that time I am reading books about western philosophy (e.g., *An Illustrated Brief History of Western Philosophy* by Anthony Kenny and *The History of Western Philosophy* by Bertrand Russell) and I am fascinated by Plato's "Theory of Forms" and want to apply this idea to my work. When I read the sentence "linguists group some words of language into classes (sets) which show similar syntactic behaviour" in Christopher Manning and Hinrich Schutze's book *Foundations of Statistical Natural Language Processing* [1], I knew I find the way to apply Plato's idea to linguistic analysis. But because there is controversy in Plato's "Theory of Forms," I use Manning and Schutze's words to describe the inspiration for my linguistic research.

After the acceptance of the SynTime paper by the 55th annual meeting of the Association for Computational Linguistics (ACL2017), I began employing learning-based methods to resolve the same task of time expression recognition. The previous version of SynTime was ever submitted to the 26th International World Wide Web Conference (WWW2017) but rejected. However, one reviewer raised two inspiring questions *"Lack of discussion on alternative (obvious approaches)—CRFs?"* and *"I was curious to understand why sequence taggers wouldn't do a good job on this task and why the authors don't think about using one.*" The two questions tell me that using conditional random fields (CRFs) for sequence tagging is obvious and even a common knowledge in this area and that previous research might have demonstrated that CRFs did not perform well on time expression recognition. Therefore, I focus on analyzing the CRFs model. During my analysis, I believe that for a task, those good results that can be achieved by rule-based methods must also be achieved by learning-based methods; if not, there must be something wrong, and as shown in Fig. 1, the problem is likely to be that model assumptions do not fit data characteristics. When we understand data characteristics well, we can always develop different models whose assumptions fit data characteristics, no matter whether these models are rule-based or learning-based; in that case, these models will achieve comparable good results. Because I have this scientific philosophy in my mind, I actually do not take much time to figure out what is wrong with the CRFs model in sequence tagging: the conventional position-based tagging schemes (e.g., the BIO and BILOU schemes) that CRFs use suffer from the problem of inconsistent tag assignment. More specifically, position-based schemes assume that time expressions are formed by fixed structure and fixed collocation. Intuitively, this is not true, because language is flexible. The problem of inconsistent tag assignment leads to a situation where the assumption of position-based tagging schemes does not fit the characteristics of data. To resolve this problem, we have to develop one or more new models that fit the data characteristics. And I define a new type of tagging schemes based on constituents rather than positions. I spend about 6 weeks to complete experiments, but the paper writing and revision cost me 3 months. In manuscript writing and revising, I think carefully about every possible aspect and every sentence, and polish them again and again until the conference deadline. After the TOMN paper [3] was accepted by WWW2018, I extended the idea of defining constituent-based tagging schemes to general named entities and write it into the UGTO paper [4].

When analyzing named entities, I find that the classical task of jointly modeling named entity recognition and classification as an end-to-end task does not make sense. I did some research and had not found any literature conducting experiments to examine the underlying assumption behind the classical task: the two sub-tasks can enhance each other under a joint modeling framework. So I conduct experiments to examine such assumption. Intuitively, named entity recognition is to recognize some chunks from unstructured text, and it is not related to semantics because we can recognize those chunks without knowing their meanings, given that training data contain enough instances targeting the chunks of interest. However, to classify those recognized chunks into different categories, we have to know their meanings. Therefore, intuitively, named entity recognition is a syntactic task which is related to the structure of text, while named entity classification is a semantic task which is related to the meaning of those chunks. Experimental results on the examination of the assumption confirm my intuition [5].

References

1. Manning C, Schutze H (1999) Foundations of statistical natural language processing. MIT Press, Cambridge
2. Zhong X (2020) Time expression and named entity analysis and recognition. PhD thesis, Nanyang Technological University, Singapore
3. Zhong X, Cambria E (2018) Time expression recognition using a constituent-based tagging scheme. In: Proceedings of the 2018 world wide web conference, Lyon, France, p 983–992
4. Zhong X, Cambria E, Hussain A (2020) Extracting time expressions and named entities with constituent-based tagging schemes. Cogn Comput 12(4):844–862
5. Zhong X, Cambria E, Hussain A (2021) Does semantics aid syntax? An empirical study on named entity recognition and classification. Neural Comput Appl

Acknowledgments

Besides Erik and Jagath, I am also thankful to Prof. Jie Zhang, Prof. Shafiq Joty, and Prof. Kezhi Mao for dedicating their precious time to serve as my thesis advisory committee, and Prof. Cuntai Guan, Prof. Xavier Bresson, and Prof. Kezhi Mao for devoting their valuable time as my thesis panel members.

I want to thank my group mates and lab mates in the Computational Intelligence Lab (CIL) and Biomedical Informatics Lab (BIL) for their companionship in the journey of pursuing knowledge and expanding the boundaries of our understanding. I would also want to thank the following language coaches in the Communication Cube (CommCube) of the Language and Communication Centre (LCC): Haoxin, Nicole, Sean, Kathryn, Daniel, Maitreya, Hilary, Terri, Paul, Christine, Gaia, Atiqah, Zhilian, Shalini, Hunter, Autumn, Izza, and Timothy. With their help, I have corrected many mistakes in my pronunciation and significantly improved my spoken English and communication skills. The staffs in the graduate student office, especially Ms. Chiam Poh Ling and Ms. Juliana Binte Jaapar, helped me a lot in various of affairs, and I am very grateful to them.

I would also want to thank the Springer Nature staffs, Dr. Celine Chang and Ms. Priya Shankar, for their kind dealing with the publication of our book and for their professional reviews and useful suggestions.

Finally, special thanks are given to my parents, Zhenhuan Zhong and Limei Xiao, for their unconditional love and support in the past 30 years, and to my honey, Han Li, for her unending love, trust, and support.

Beijing, China   Xiaoshi Zhong
1 August 2021

Contents

Acronyms and Notations

TER	Time expression recognition
TEN	Time expression normalization
TERN	Time expression and normalization
NER	Named entity recognition
NEC	Named entity classification
NERC	Named entity recognition and classification
CRFs	Conditional random fields
POS	Part of speech
SynTime	Our type-based method for time expression recognition
TOMN	Our learning-based method for time expression recognition
TOMN Scheme	Our constituent-based tagging scheme that TOMN defines to model time expressions
UGTO	Our learning-based method for named entity recognition
UGTO Scheme	Our constituent-based tagging scheme that UGTO defines to model named entities

List of Figures

List of Tables

Chapter 1
Introduction

Abstract This book presents our analysis of intrinsic characteristics of time expressions and named entities, and our use of these characteristics to design algorithms to recognize time expressions and named entities from unstructured text. Regarding time expressions, we find their five common characteristics from four diverse datasets, and according to these characteristics, we propose two methods to model time expressions. The first method is a type-based method termed SynTime, which defines three main syntactic *token types* to group time-related token regular expressions, and designs a small set of general *heuristic rules* to recognize time expressions. Our second method is a learning-based method termed TOMN, which defines a constituent-based tagging scheme with four tags, indicating four types of constituent words of time expressions. Essentially, our TOMN scheme overcomes the problem of *inconsistent tag assignment* that is caused by the conventional *position-based tagging schemes*. Regarding named entities, we find their three common characteristics from two benchmark datasets, and these characteristics motivate us to design a CRFs-based learning method termed UGTO to model named entities. Like TOMN, UGTO defines another constituent-based tagging scheme with four tags, indicating four types of constituent words of named entities, and the UGTO scheme overcomes the problem of inconsistent tag assignment. When analyzing named entities, we find that named entity recognition is a syntactic task while named entity classification is a semantic task; and the classical task of jointly modeling named entity recognition and classification as an end-to-end task does not improve the performance of the single named entity recognition.

Keywords Time expressions · Named entities · Intrinsic characteristics ·
Token types · Heuristic rules · Inconsistent tag assignment · Position-based
tagging scheme · Constituent-based tagging schemes · Syntactic task ·
Semantic task

Time expressions and named entities play important roles in the fields of data mining, information retrieval, and natural language processing [9, 21, 35, 43, 54, 55, 68]. They are involved in many linguistic tasks, such as temporal relation extraction [7, 36, 65], timeline construction [15, 31, 39], temporal information retrieval [1, 6], named entity recognition and classification [10, 21, 54], named entity typing [20, 32, 44], entity linking [24, 33], domain-specific entity recognition [27, 45, 63, 69], relation extraction and reasoning [40, 70, 71], and many others.

Researchers from various areas have devoted tremendous effort for more than two decades to specify standards for the annotations of time expressions [18, 48, 50, 59] and named entities [10, 11, 16, 21, 53, 54], construct annotated corpora for the analyses of time expressions [38, 49, 59, 74] and named entities [10, 11, 14, 16, 21, 46, 47, 52–54, 57, 67], and recognize time expressions and named entities from unstructured text [3–5, 9, 16, 21, 53, 54, 64–66].

To better understand their intrinsic characteristics, we analyze four diverse datasets about time expressions and two benchmark datasets about named entities, and summarize some of their common characteristics. According to these characteristics, we propose two models to recognize time expressions and one model to recognize named entities from unstructured text [72–76].

1.1   Time Expression Analysis and Recognition

The four datasets we use to analyze time expressions are TimeBank [49], TE3-Silver [64], WikiWars [38], and Tweets [74]. From our analysis we summarize five common characteristics about time expressions. Firstly, most time expressions are very short, with more than 80% of time expressions containing no more than three words. Secondly, most time expressions contain time tokens that can distinguish time expressions from common text; more than 91.8% of time expressions containing at least one time tokens while no more than 0.7% of common text containing time tokens. Thirdly, those words that are used to express time information are in a small size, with only about 70 distinct time tokens in an individual dataset and about 120 distinct time tokens across all the four datasets. Fourthly, similar constituent words in time expressions demonstrate similar syntactic behaviours. Finally, time expressions are formed by loose structure, with more than 53.5% of distinct time tokens appearing in different positions within time expressions. The first four characteristics are related to the principle of least effort [77], which states that at both individual and collective level, people tend to act under the least effort in order to minimize the cost of energy in almost all the aspects of human actions, including language use. Time expressions are part of language and act as an interface of communication. Short expressions, occurrence and distinction, small vocabulary, and similar syntactic behaviour all reduce the cost of our energy required to communicate with each other. The last characteristic demonstrates the flexibility of time expressions.

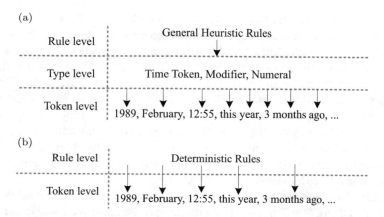

Fig. 1.1 Key differences between SynTime and other rule-based time taggers. (**a**) Layout of SynTime. The layout consists of three levels: token level, type level, and rule level. Token types group the constituent words of time expressions. Heuristic rules work on token types in a heuristic manner and are independent of specific tokens and therefore SynTime is independent of specific domains, text types, and even languages. (**b**) Layout of other rule-based time taggers. The layout mainly consists of two levels: token level and rule level. Deterministic rules work directly on tokens and phrases in a fixed manner and therefore other rule-based time taggers lack flexibility

According to these five characteristics we propose two methods to recognize time expressions from unstructured text. Our first method is a type-based method termed SynTime ("Syn" stands for "syntactic"). SynTime defines three main token types, namely *time token*, *modifier*, and *numeral*, to group time-related token regular expressions. Time tokens include those words that explicitly express time information, such as time units (e.g., "month" and "year"). Modifiers modify time tokens and appear around them; for example, the two modifiers "several" and "ago" modify the time token "year" in the time expression "several years ago." Numerals include ordinals and numbers (except those tokens that are identified as YEAR, e.g., "2006"). From raw text, SynTime firstly identifies time tokens, then recognizes modifiers and numerals, and finally recognize full time expressions.

Naturally, SynTime is a also rule-based tagger. The key differences between SynTime and other rule-based time expression taggers lie in the ways of how to define token types and how to design rules (see Fig. 1.1a, b). The definition of token types in SynTime is inspired by the part-of-speech (POS) of language, in which "linguists group some words of language into classes (sets) which show similar syntactic behaviour" [37]. SynTime defines token types for tokens according to their syntactic behaviours. Other rule-based taggers define token types for tokens based on their semantic meanings. For example, SUTime defines five semantic modifier types, such as frequency modifiers and approximate modifiers,[1] while SynTime defines five syntactic modifier types, such as modifiers that appear before

---

[1] https://github.com/stanfordnlp/CoreNLP/tree/master/src/edu/stanford/nlp/time/rules.

time tokens and modifiers that appear after time tokens (see Sect. 4.1 for details). Accordingly, other rule-based taggers design deterministic rules working directly on tokens themselves. SynTime instead designs general rules working on token types rather than on tokens themselves. For example, our general rules do not work on the tokens "February" and "1989" but work on their token types "MONTH" and "YEAR." That is why we call SynTime a type-based method. More importantly, other rule-based taggers design rules in a fixed manner, including fixed length and fixed position. By contrast, SynTime designs general rules in a heuristic way based on the idea of boundary expansion. Therefore, SynTime is much more flexible than other rule-based methods. Furthermore, these general heuristic rules are quite light-weight, which leads SynTime to run in real time.

Since our heuristic rules are designed to work on token types and are independent of specific tokens, SynTime is independent of specific domains, specific text types, and even specific languages that consists of specific tokens. In this book, we test SynTime on specific domains and specific text types in English. Testing on other languages needs to construct a collection of token regular expressions in target languages under our defined token types or other token-type systems.

Our second method is a learning-based method termed TOMN. Specifically, TOMN defines a constituent-based tagging scheme termed TOMN scheme consisting of four tags, namely T, O, M, and N, indicating the constituent words of time expressions and corresponding the three main token types defined in SynTime, namely *time token*, *modifier*, *numeral*, and those words appearing *outside* time expressions.[2] In practice, TOMN models time expressions under a CRFs framework [28] with only a kind of TOMN pre-tag features and lemma features. During modeling and tagging, it assigns a word with one of the four TOMN tags.

The TOMN scheme can keep tag assignment consistent during training and therefore overcomes the problem of inconsistent tag assignment that is caused by conventional position-based tagging schemes.[3] The loose structure by which time expressions are formed exhibits in the following two aspects. Firstly, many time expressions consist of loose collocations. For example, the time token "September" can form a time expression by itself, or forms "September 2006" by another time token appearing after it, or forms "1 September 2006" by a numeral appearing before it and another time token appearing after it. Secondly, some time expressions can change their word order without changing their meanings. For example, "September 2006" can be written as "2006 September" without changing its meaning. The conventional tagging schemes like BILOU [51] are based on *the positions within a labeled chunk*, namely a unit-word chunk, and the beginning, inside, and last word of a multi-word chunk. Under the BILOU scheme, a word

---

[2]We use "TOMN" to denote our method for time expression recognition while use "TOMN scheme" to denote the constituent-based tagging scheme that TOMN defines to model time expressions.

[3]In a supervised-learning procedure, tag assignment occurs in two stages: (1) feature extraction in the training stage and (2) tag prediction in the testing stage. We focus on the training stage to analyze the impact of tag assignment.

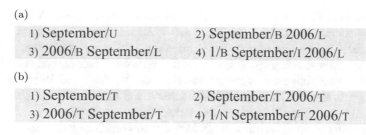

(a)
  1) September/U   2) September/B 2006/L
  3) 2006/B September/L   4) 1/B September/I 2006/L

(b)
  1) September/T   2) September/T 2006/T
  3) 2006/T September/T   4) 1/N September/T 2006/T

Fig. 1.2 Comparison of tag assignments under the BILOU scheme and our TOMN scheme. The BILOU scheme is based on the positions within labeled chunks, while our TOMN scheme is based on the constituent words of labeled chunks. Here, *inconsistent tag assignment* is defined as that during training, a word is assigned with different tags simply because this word appears in different positions within labeled chunks. (**a**) Tag assignment under the BILOU scheme: "September" in different positions within labeled time expressions is assigned with different tags of U, B, L, or I. The inconsistent tag assignment reduces the predictive power of "September," and this contradicts the characteristic that time tokens can distinguish time expressions from common text. (**b**) Tag assignment under our TOMN scheme: "September" in different positions within labeled time expressions is consistently assigned with the same tag of T. The consistent tag assignment protects the predictive power of "September" and avoids potential tag balance (The definition of inconsistent tag assignment can be generalized as that during training, a unit in different labeled instances is assigned with different tags for some reason(s) while that unit should be consistently assigned with a same tag. The unit of interest can be a word, a phrase, a sentence, an article, a relation, a webpage, or a group of words as a whole, etc.)

that appears in different positions within labeled time expressions is assigned with different tags; for example, the above time token "September" can be assigned with U, B, L, or I (see Fig. 1.2a). Such inconsistent tag assignment causes difficulty for statistical models to model time expressions. Firstly, inconsistent tag assignment reduces the predictive power of lexicon, and this contradicts the characteristic we find that time tokens can distinguish time expressions from common text. Secondly, inconsistent tag assignment might cause the problem of tag imbalance. By contrast, Our TOMN scheme is based on *the constituents of a labeled chunk* (i.e., time token, modifier, and numeral) and assigns the same constituent word with the same tag, regardless of its frequency and its positions within time expressions. Under our TOMN scheme, for example, the above time token "September" is consistently assigned with T (see Fig. 1.2b). With such consistent tag assignment, our TOMN scheme protects the predictive power of time tokens and avoids the potential problem of tag imbalance.

We evaluate the quality of SynTime and TOMN against four state-of-the-art methods (i.e., HeidelTime [58], SUTime [8], ClearTK [2], and UWTime [30]) on three diverse datasets (i.e., TE-3 [64], WikiWars [38], and Tweets).[4] HeidelTime and SUTime are rule-based methods while ClearTK and UWTime are learning-

---

[4]The TE3-Silver dataset is only used in our analysis for the characteristics of time expressions; it is not used in our experiments because the labels of its time expressions are not ground-truth labels but instead are automatically generated by other time expression taggers.

based methods. TE-3 and Tweets are comprehensive datasets while WikiWars is a domain-specific dataset about war. TE-3 and WikiWars are datasets in formal text while Tweets is in informal text. Experimental results demonstrate that SynTime and TOMN achieve comparable results on the WikiWars dataset, and significantly outperform these four state-of-the-art baselines on the TE-3 and Tweets datasets. More importantly, SynTime and TOMN achieve the best recalls on all the three datasets and exceptionally good results on the Tweets dataset. Experimental results also demonstrate the robustness of TOMN on cross-dataset experiments against the two learning-based baselines and demonstrate the advantage of our constituent-based tagging scheme against the conventional position-based tagging schemes.

1.2 Named Entity Analysis and Recognition

The two datasets we use to analyze named entities are CoNLL03 [54] and OntoNotes* (OntoNotes* is a derived version of the OntoNotes5 corpus [46, 47]; see Sect. 3.2.1 for details). From our analysis we find three common characteristics about named entities. Firstly, most named entities contain uncommon words, with more than 92.2% of named entities have at least one word hardly appearing in common text. Secondly, named entities are mainly made up of proper nouns; in the whole text, more than 84.8% of proper nouns appear in named entities, and within named entities, more than 80.1% of words are proper nouns. Thirdly, named entities are formed by loose structure, with more than 53.77% of distinct words appearing in different positions within named entities.

These three characteristics motivate us to design a CRFs-based learning method termed UGTO to recognize named entities from unstructured text. Specifically, UGTO defines a constituent-based tagging scheme termed UGTO scheme that consists of four tags: U, G, T, and O.[5] The UGTO scheme is designed to encode the constituent words of named entities. Specifically, U encodes *uncommon words* and entity-related tokens, such as "Boston" and "Africans." G encodes *generic modifiers* while T encodes *trigger words*. Generic modifiers (e.g., "of" and "and") can appear in several types of named entities while trigger words appear in a specific type of named entities; for example, the trigger word "University" appears in the ORG named entities "Boston University" and "Stanford University." O encodes those words that appear *outside* named entities. In modeling, UGTO assigns a word with a UGTO tag under a CRFs framework with only UGTO pre-tag features, a kind of word cluster features, and some basic lexical and POS features (see Sect. 6.1.4.1 for details).

---

[5]Similar to the use of "TOMN" and "TOMN scheme," we use "UGTO" to denote our proposed method for named entity recognition while use "UGTO scheme" to denote the constituent-based tagging scheme that UGTO defines to model named entities.

UGTO extends the idea of TOMN from time expression modeling to named entity modeling. Like TOMN, UGTO overcomes the problem of inconsistent tag assignment and therefore fully leverages the information of uncommon words and proper nouns. The key difference between UGTO and TOMN lies in the difference between general named entities and time expressions. Firstly, time expressions contain only a small group of time-related words, which can be wholly collected (e.g., only 350 unique words appear in time expressions across the four analyzed datasets). By contrast, general named entities contain countless words, and it is difficult to collect all of them (e.g., 23,698 unique words appear in named entities across the two analyzed datasets). Secondly, POS tags cannot distinguish time expressions from common text and TOMN does not take into account any syntactic features. However, named entities are mainly made of proper nouns, which are a kind of syntactic features, and proper nouns are important information that is used in UGTO. In practice, UGTO derives two kinds of uncommon words from annotated training set and unannotated test set based on the idea that those words that hardly appear in the common text of the training set are likely to predict named entities (see Fig. 6.1 for details of the idea).

We evaluate the quality of UGTO on two benchmark datasets (i.e., CoNLL03 [54] and OntoNotes* [46]) against two representative state-of-the-art baselines (StanfordNERC [19] and LSTM-CRF [29]). CoNLL03 is a small dataset collected from news articles in formal text, while OntoNotes* is a large-scale datasets collected from diverse sources over a long period of time. StanfordNERC is used as the representative of traditional hand-crafted-feature methods while LSTM-CRF is as the representative of recent auto-learned-feature methods. Experimental results demonstrate the effectiveness and efficiency of UGTO against these two representative baselines. Experimental results also demonstrate that traditional hand-crafted-feature methods can achieve state-of-the-art performance on named entity recognition, in comparison with the state-of-the-art auto-learned-feature method, and that joint modeling named entity recognition and classification does not improve the performance of named entity recognition, in both our model and these two representative baselines (see Sect. 6.3.3 for details).

1.3   Does Semantics Aid Syntax?

In the fields of computational linguistics and natural language processing, researchers usually model multiple tasks simultaneously without realizing they implicitly assume that these individual tasks can enhance each other under a joint optimization framework. Sometimes such multiple modeling attempts achieve good results, but sometimes these attempts fail. For example, the joint modeling of syntactic and semantic parsings aims to simultaneously formulate both the syntactic parsing and semantic parsing under a framework, but such joint modeling tasks cannot improve the performance of single task; what is even worse, the joint modeling tasks hurt the single task [22, 23, 25, 34, 56, 60–62]. Another famous joint modeling task goes to the classic named entity recognition and classification (NERC), which aims to jointly model named entity recognition (NER) and named entity classification (NEC) as an end-to-end task [10, 21, 54], assuming that NER and NEC can enhance each other under a joint optimization framework. However, there is no existing literature that examines whether such implicit assumption is true or not; perhaps these researchers have not yet realized that they make such implicit assumption in those joint modeling tasks.

In this book, we aim to examine whether a semantic task can improve the performance of a syntactic task. To this end, we specify the way to determine whether a linguistic task is a syntactic task or a semantic task according to Chomsky's syntactic theory [12, 13] and Katz and Fodor's foundation of semantic theory [17, 26, 41, 42] (see Sect. 6.2 for details). To land down our goal in practice, we conduct our examination on a classical linguistic task, namely NERC, which contains two sub-tasks: NER and NEC.

A line of research on NEC (also known as named entity typing) reports that semantic information is much more effective than syntactic information for NEC [20, 32, 44]. This indicates, according to our specification of syntactic tasks and semantic tasks described in Sect. 6.2, that NEC is a semantic task. In this paper, therefore, we focus on NER, and aim to empirically examine the following two questions: (1) whether can the joint NERC task improve the NER performance? (2) whether NER is a syntactic task?

To answer these questions, we further conduct extensive experiments on the two well-known benchmark datasets, namely CoNLL03 [54] and OntoNotes* by using our UGTO model and the two representative state-of-the-art models, namely StanfordNERC [19] and LSTM-CRF [29]. Refer to Sect. 6.3.2 for our four designed experiments. Experimental results demonstrate that (1) the joint NERC task does not improve the NER performance, (2) NER is not a semantic task but a syntactic task, and (3) semantic information does not further improve the NER performance [76]. This suggests us to separately address the two sub-tasks of NER and NEC, and further suggests us as well that before we conduct research on simultaneously modeling multiple linguistic tasks, we should examine whether these multiple tasks could enhance each other.

Although our analysis and experiments demonstrate that neither the NEC task alone nor the joint NERC task can further improve the NER performance, there are still some potential limitations in our work that require to be resolved in the future. One limitation is that our analysis on the NER and NEC tasks is just an empirical case of examining whether semantics or semantic information can improve the performance of a syntactic task. To fully examine the proposition of whether semantics can aid syntax, we still need to examine many other syntactic tasks such as syntactic parsing to see whether semantics or semantic information could improve those syntactic tasks. In the future, we will continue such kinds of examinations to justify the validity or invalidity of this proposition. Another limitation is that although our experiment are designed to learn syntactic information or semantic information from context, we could not guarantee that those models learn only the syntactic information without learning any semantic information, nor that those models learn only the semantic information without learning any syntactic information. What is even worse, it is still not clear whether we could separate syntactic information from semantic information. In the future, we will also try to resolve these issues.

1.4 Organization of This Book

The structure of this book is organized as follows.

In Chap. 1, we summarize the content of this book and our contributions, including (1) the analysis of intrinsic characteristics of time expressions and named entities, (2) two methods for time expression recognition and one method for named entity recognition, and (3) our empirical justification that the classical task of joint modeling of named entity recognition and classification does not improve the performance of the named entity recognition.

In Chap. 2, we overview the literature about time expression recognition and normalization, named entity recognition and classification, and those research that involves joint modeling of multiple syntactic and semantic tasks.

In Chap. 3, we detail our analysis on four diverse datasets for intrinsic characteristics of time expressions and two benchmark datasets for intrinsic characteristics of named entities as well as our summarized common characteristics about time expressions and named entities.

In Chap. 4, we detail our type-based time tagger, SynTime, which defines syntactic token types and design general heuristic rules to recognize time expressions from unstructured text, and the evaluation that we conduct on three datasets to justify the effectiveness of SynTime in comparison with both rule-based and learning-based state-of-the-art models.

In Chap. 5, we detail our proposed CRFs-based learning time tagger, TOMN, which defines a constituent-based tagging scheme to model time expressions under the framework of conditional random fields with minimal features, and the evaluation that we conduct on three datasets to justify the effectiveness, efficiency, and robustness of TOMN against both rule-based and learning-based state-of-the-art models.

In Chap. 6, we detail our proposed CRFs-based learning method, UGTO, which defines another constituent-based tagging scheme with minimal features to model named entities, as well as the experiments we conduct on two benchmark datasets to justify the effectiveness of UGTO in comparison with two representative state-of-the-art models. We also detail the evaluation that is conducted to justify that named entity recognition is a syntactic task and the joint modeling of NERC does not improve the NER performance under a joint modeling framework.

In Chap. 7, we draw a conclusion about this book and outline some potential directions in future research.

References

1. Alonso O, Strotgen J, Baeza-Yates R, Gertz M (2011) Temporal information retrieval: challenges and opportunities. In: Proceedings of 1st international temporal web analytics workshop, p 1–8
2. Bethard S (2013) Cleartk-timeml: a minimalist approach to TempEval 2013. In: Proceedings of the 7th international workshop on semantic evaluation, p 10–14
3. Bethard S, Derczynski L, Savova G, Pustejovsky J, Verhagen M (2015) Semeval-2015 task 6: clinical TempEval. In: Proceedings of the 9th international workshop on semantic evaluation, p 806–814
4. Bethard S, Savova G, Chen WT, Derczynski L, Pustejovsky J, Verhagen M (2016) Semeval-2016 task 12: clinical TempEval. In: Proceedings of the 10th international workshop on semantic evaluation, p 1052–1062
5. Bethard S, Savova G, Palmer M, Pustejovsky J (2017) Semeval-2017 task 12: clinical tempeval. In: Proceedings of the 11th international workshop on semantic evaluation, p 565–572
6. Campos R, Dias G, Jorge AM, Jatowt A (2014) Survey of temporal information retrieval and related applications. ACM Comput Surv 47(2):15:1–41
7. Chambers N, Wang S, Jurafsky D (2007) Classifying temporal relations between events. In: Proceedings of the 45th annual meeting of the ACL on interactive poster and demonstration sessions, p 173–176
8. Chang AX, Manning CD (2012) Sutime: a library for recognizing and normalizing time expressions. In: Proceedings of 8th international conference on language resources and evaluation, p 3735–3740
9. Chinchor NA (1997) MUC-7 named entity task definition. In: Proceedings of the 7th message understanding conference, vol 29
10. Chinchor NA (1998) MUC-7 named entity task definition. In: Proceedings of the 7th message understanding conference, vol 29
11. Chinchor NA (1998) Overview of MUC-7/MET-2. In: Proceedings of the 7th message understanding conference
12. Chomsky N (1957) Syntactic structures. Mouton Publishers, Berlin
13. Chomsky N (1965) Aspects of the theory of syntax. MIT Press, Cambridge
14. Derczynski L, Bontcheva K, Roberts I (2016) Broad twitter corpus: a diverse named entity recognition resource. In: Proceedings of the 26th international conference on computational linguistics, p 1169–1179
15. Do QX, Lu W, Roth D (2012) Joint inference for event timeline construction. In: Proceedings of the 2012 joint conference on empirical methods in natural language processing and computational natural language learning, p 677–687
16. Doddington G, Mitchell A, Przybocki M, Ramshaw L, Strassel S, Weischedel R (2004) The automatic content extraction (ace) program tasks, data, and evaluation. In: Proceedings of the 2004 conference on language resources and evaluation, p 1–4
17. Dowty DR, Wall RE, Peters S (1981) Introduction to montague semantics. Dordrecht, Reidel
18. Ferro L, Gerber L, Mani I, Sundheim B, Wilson G (2005) Tides 2005 standard for the annotation of temporal expressions. Tech. rep., MITRE
19. Finkel JR, Grenager T, Manning C (2005) Incorporating non-local information into information extraction systems by Gibbs sampling. In: Proceedings of the 43nd annual meeting of the association for computational linguistics, p 363–370
20. Giuliano C (2009) Fine-grained classification of named entities exploiting latent semantic kernels. In: CoNLL
21. Grishman R, Sundheim B (1996) Message understanding conference—6: a brief history. In: Proceedings of the 16th international conference on computational linguistics
22. Hajič J, Ciaramita M, Johansson R, Kawahara D, Martí MA, Màrquez L, Meyers A, Nivre J, Padó S, Štěpánek P, Surdeanu M, Xue N, Zhang Y (2009) The CoNLL-2009 shared task: syntactic and semantic dependencies in multiple languages. In: Proceedings of the 13th conference on computational natural language learning, p 1–18

23. Henderson J, Merlo P, Titov I, Musillo G (2013) Multilingual joint parsing of syntactic and semantic dependencies with a latent variable model. Comput Linguist 39(4):949–998
24. Ji H, Grishman R (2011) Knowledge base population: successful approaches and challenges. In: Proceedings of the 49th annual meeting of the association for computational linguistics, p 1148–1158
25. Johansson R, Nugues P (2008) Dependency-based syntactic-semantic analysis with Propbank and Nombank. In: Proceedings of the 12th conference on computational natural language learning, p 183–187
26. Katz JJ, Fodor JA (1963) The structure of a semantic theory. Language 39(2):170–210
27. Krallinger M, Leitner F, Rabal O, Vazquez M, Oyarzabal J, Valencia A (2015) Overview of the chemical compound and drug name recognition (CHEMDNER) task. In: BioCreative challenge evaluation workshop, vol 2, p 2–33
28. Lafferty J, McCallum A, Pereira F (2001) Conditional random fields: probabilistic models for segmenting and labeling sequence data. In: Proceedings of the 18th international conference on machine learning, p 281–289
29. Lample G, Ballesteros M, Subramanian S, Kawakami K, Dyer C (2016) Neural architecture for named entity recognition. In: Proceedings of the 15th annual conference of the North American chapter of the association for computational linguistics, p 260–270
30. Lee K, Artzi Y, Dodge J, Zettlemoyer L (2014) Context-dependent semantic parsing for time expressions. In: Proceedings of the 52th annual meeting of the association for computational linguistics, p 1437–1447
31. Li J, Cardie C (2014) Timeline generation: tracking individuals on twitter. In: Proceedings of the 23rd international conference on world wide web, p 643–652
32. Ling X, Weld DS (2012) Fine-grained entity recognition. In: Proceedings of the twenty-sixth conference on artificial intelligence
33. Ling X, Singh S, Weld DS (2015) Design challenges for entity linking. Trans Assoc Comput Linguist 3:315–328
34. Lluís X, Carreras X, Màrquez L (2013) Joint arc-factored parsing of syntactic and semantic dependencies. Trans Assoc Comput Linguist 1:219–230
35. Mani I (2003) Recent developments in temporal information. In: Proceedings of the international conference on recent advances in natural language processing, p 45–60
36. Mani I, Verhagen M, Wellner B, Lee CM, Pustejovsky J (2006) Machine learning of temporal relations. In: Proceedings of the 21st international conference on computational linguistics and the 44th annual meeting of the association for computational linguistics, p 753–760
37. Manning C, Schutze H (1999) Foundations of statistical natural language processing. MIT Press, Cambridge
38. Mazur P, Dale R (2010) Wikiwars: a new corpus for research on temporal expressions. In: Proceedings of the 2010 Conference on empirical methods in natural language processing, pp 913–922
39. Minard AL, Speranza M, Agirre E, Aldabe I, van Erp M, Magnini B, Rigau G, Urizar R (2015) Semeval-2015 task 4: timeline: cross-document event ordering. In: 9th international workshop on semantic evaluation (SemEval 2015), p 778–786
40. Mintz M, Bills S, Snow R, Jurafsky D (2009) Distant supervision for relation extraction without labeled data. In: Proceedings of the 47th annual meeting of the ACL and the 4th IJCNLP of the AFNLP, Singapore, p 1003–1011
41. Montague R (1970) Universal grammar. Theoria 36:373–398
42. Montague R (1973) The proper treatment of quantification in ordinary English. Approaches to Nat Lang p 221–242
43. Nadeau D, Sekine S (2007) A survey of named entity recognition and classification. Lingvisticae Investigationes 30(1):3–26
44. Nakashole N, Tylenda T, Weikum G (2013) Fine-grained semantic typing of emerging entities. In: Proceedings of the 51st annual meeting of the association for computational linguistics, p 1488–1497

45. Patrick J, Li M (2010) High accuracy information extraction of medication information from clinical notes: 2009 i2b2 medication extraction challenge. J Am Med Inform Assoc 17(5):524–527
46. Pradhan S, Moschitti A, Xue N, Ng HT, Bjorkelund A, Uryupina O, Zhang Y, Zhong Z (2013) Towards robust linguistic analysis using ontonotes. In: Proceedings of the 7th conference on computational natural language learning, p 143–152
47. Pradhan SS, Hovy E, Marcus M, Palmer M, Ramshaw L, Weischedel R (2007) Ontonotes: a unified relational semantic representation. In: Proceedings of the 2007 ieee international conference on semantic computing, p 517–526
48. Pustejovsky J, Castano J, Ingria R, Sauri R, Gaizauskas R, Setzer A, Katz G, Radev D (2003) Timeml: robust specification of event and temporal expressions in text. New Dir Quest Answering 3:28–34
49. Pustejovsky J, Hanks P, Sauri R, See A, Gaizauskas R, Setzer A, Sundheim B, Radev D, Day D, Ferro L, Lazo M (2003) The timebank corpus. Corpus Linguist 2003:647–656
50. Pustejovsky J, Lee K, Bunt H, Romary L (2010) ISO-TimeML: an international standard for semantic annotation. In: Proceedings of the seventh conference on international language resources and evaluation (LREC'10), p 394–397
51. Ratinov L, Roth D (2009) Design challenges and misconceptions in named entity recognition. In: Proceedings of the thirteenth conference on computational natural language learning, p 147–155
52. Ritter A, Clark S, Mausam, Etzioni O (2011) Named entity recognition in tweets: an experimental study. In: Proceedings of the 2011 conference on empirical methods in natural language processing, p 1524–1534
53. Sang EFTK (2002) Introduction to the CoNLL-2002 shared task: language-independent named entity recognition. In: Proceedings of the 6th conference on natural language learning
54. Sang EFTK, Meulder FD (2003) Introduction to the CoNLL-2003 shared task: language-independent named entity recognition. In: Proceedings of the 7th conference on natural language learning, pp 142–147
55. Sekine S, Ranchhod E (2009) Named entities: recognition, classification and use, vol 19
56. Shi P, Zhang Y (2017) Joint bi-affine parsing and semantic role labeling. In: Proceedings of the 2017 international conference on Asian language processing, p 338–341
57. Strauss B, Toma BE, Ritter A, de Marneffe MC, Xu W (2016) Results of the WNUT16 named entity recognition shared task. In: Proceedings of the 2nd workshop on noisy user-generated text, p 138–144
58. Strötgen J, Gertz M (2010) Heideltime: high quality rule-based extraction and normalization of temporal expressions. In: Proceedings of the 5th international workshop on semantic evaluation (SemEval'10), Association for Computational Linguistics, Stroudsburg, p 321–324
59. Styler IV WF, Bethard S, Finan S, Palmer M, Pradhan S, De Groen PC, Erickson B, Miller T, Lin C, Savova G, Pustejovsky J (2014) Temporal annotation in the clinical domain. Trans Assoc Comput Linguist 2:143–154
60. Surdeanu M, Johansson R, Meyers A, Màrquez L, Nivre J (2008) The CoNLL-2008 shared task on joint parsing of syntactic and semantic dependencies. In: Proceedings of the 12th conference on computational natural language learning, p 159–177
61. Sutton C, McCallum A (2005) Joint parsing and semantic role labeling. In: Proceedings of the 9th conference on computational natural language learning, p 225–229
62. Swayamdipta S, Ballesteros M, Dyer C, Smith NA (2016) Greedy, joint syntactic-semantic parsing with stack LSTMs. In: Proceedings of the 20th SIGNLL conference on computational natural language learning, p 187–197
63. Takeuchi K, Collier N (2005) Bio-medical entity extraction using support vector machines. Artif Intell Med 33(2):125–137
64. UzZaman N, Llorens H, Derczynski L, Verhagen M, Allen J, Pustejovsky J (2013) Semeval-2013 task 1: TempEval-3: evaluating time expressions, events, and temporal relations. In: Proceedings of the 7th international workshop on semantic evaluation, p 1–9

65. Verhagen M, Gaizauskas R, Schilder F, Hepple M, Katz G, Pustejovsky J (2007) Semeval-2007 task 15: TempEval temporal relation identification. In: Proceedings of the 4th international workshop on semantic evaluation, p 75–80

66. Verhagen M, Sauri R, Caselli T, Pustejovsky J (2010) Semeval-2010 task 13: TempEval-2. In: Proceedings of the 5th international workshop on semantic evaluation, p 57–62

67. Weischedel R, Brunstein A (2005) BBN pronoun conference and entity type corpus. In: Linguistic data consortium, vol 112

68. Wong KF, Xia Y, Li W, Yuan C (2005) An overview of temporal information extraction. Int J Comput Process Orient Lang 18(2):137–152

69. Xia Y, Zhong X, Liu P, Tan C, Na S, Hu Q, Huang Y (2013) Combining metamap and cTAKES in disorder recognition: THCIB at clef ehealth lab 2013 task 1. In: Working notes for CLEF 2013 conference

70. Zelenko D, Aone C, Richardella A (2003) Kernel methods for relation extraction. J Mach Learn Res 3:1083–1106

71. Zhong X (2013) A wikipedia based hybrid ranking method for taxonomic relation extraction. In: Proceedings of the 9th asia information retrieval societies conference, Singapore, p 332–343

72. Zhong X (2020) Time expression and named entity analysis and recognition. PhD thesis, Nanyang Technological University, Singapore

73. Zhong X, Cambria E (2018) Time expression recognition using a constituent-based tagging scheme. In: Proceedings of the 2018 world wide web conference, Lyon, France, p 983–992

74. Zhong X, Sun A, Cambria E (2017) Time expression analysis and recognition using syntactic token types and general heuristic rules. In: Proceedings of the 55th annual meeting of the association for computational linguistics, Vancouver, vol 1, p 420–429

75. Zhong X, Cambria E, Hussain A (2020) Extracting time expressions and named entities with constituent-based tagging schemes. Cogn Comput 12(4):844–862

76. Zhong X, Cambria E, Hussain A (2021) Does semantics aid syntax? An empirical study on named entity recognition and classification. Neural Comput Appl

77. Zipf G (1949) Human behavior and the principle of least effort: an introduction to human ecology. Addison-Wesley Press, Reading

Chapter 2
Literature Review

Abstract Time expressions and named entities play important roles in data mining, natural language processing, and cognitive computation. Researchers from these areas have devoted considerable effort in the last two decades to define the problem of time expression analysis, design the standards for time expression annotation, build annotated corpora for time expressions, and develop methods to identify time expressions from free text. In this literature review, we go through the previous works, aiming to draw an overview of the development of time expression and named entity analysis in different aspects, such as language factor, domain and textual type, types of time expressions, and the evaluation and resources for the time expression analysis as well as methods that researchers develop for time expression recognition and normalization, named entity recognition and classification. In addition, we also review the development of jointly modeling multiple syntactic and semantic tasks.

Keywords Time expressions · Named entities · Rule-based methods · Learning-based methods · Syntactic tasks · Semantic tasks

The works that are related to this book mainly include the research of time expression recognition and normalization [12–14, 43, 100, 120, 122, 147, 159, 162, 163, 177, 178], named entity recognition and classification [27, 53, 109, 128, 171], and those research that involves joint modeling of multiple syntactic and semantic tasks, such as joint syntactic and semantic parsings [56, 68, 151, 152].

X. Zhong, E. Cambria, *Time Expression and Named Entity Recognition*,
Socio-Affective Computing 10, https://doi.org/10.1007/978-3-030-78961-9_2

2.1   Time Expression Recognition and Normalization

The extensive studies of time expressions start from the sixth and seventh Message Understanding Conference (MUC-6 and MUC-7), in which Grishman and Sundheim [53] and Chinchor [27, 28] formally define the task of identifying time expressions from unstructured text, together with the tasks of identifying entity names and number expressions as well as other information extraction tasks. After MUC-6 and MUC-7, researchers from different fields (e.g., data mining, information retrieval, natural language processing, and related areas) have devoted tremendous effort to the analysis of time expressions [2, 22, 96, 166], specifying annotation standards for time expression [11, 41–43, 75, 98, 120, 122, 147], developing annotated corpora for time expression [100, 121, 147, 149], and organizing shared tasks to address the problems of recognizing and normalizing time expressions from unstructured text [12–14, 27, 28, 76, 112, 149, 159, 162, 163].

2.1.1   Language Factor

The majority of research in the time expression analysis is devoted to the study of English [12–14, 27, 43, 73, 75, 76, 100, 112, 120–122, 147, 159, 162, 163]. Besides English, Chinese is well studied and presented in English and Chinese literature [59, 60, 80, 167–169, 172]. Similarly, French, Italian, and Korean are strongly represented and boosted in series of works [8, 16, 23, 64–66, 77, 82, 95, 107, 160]. Many other languages receive attention as well: Arabic [19], Basque [3], Catalan [157], Croatian [137], Dutch [21], German [141], Portuguese [7, 35], Romanian [49], Spanish [130, 132, 144, 157], Swedish [9], Uyghur [108], Ukrainian [52], and Vietnamese [145]. Some works consider this problem in multilingual text [89, 113, 131, 143–145, 157, 165]. SynTime and TOMN focus on time expressions in English, and in the future, we plan to analyze time expressions in some other languages.

2.1.2   Domain and Textual Type Factor

The investigation of time expressions involves a variety of domains and textual types. The very first studies mainly focus the problem in formal text like news articles [17, 27, 121, 134]. Later on, these studies are gradually concerned with the problem in other domains and textual types. Mazur and Dale collect English articles from Wikipedia about famous wars and annotate the time expressions for domain-specific time expression analysis; this collected corpus is called WikiWars [100]. Similarly, Strotgen and Gertz develop the WikiWarsDE, which includes time expressions in the war domain collected from Wikipedia articles in German [141]. Strotgen and Gertz analyze time expressions in the texts from colloquial short message service (SMS) and scientific biomedical documents [142] while Degaetano-Ortlieb and Strotgen analyze time expressions in the scientific literature and their diachronic variation over a time span of about 350 years [36]. Tabassum et al. analyze time expressions in the tweets which are informal text [155]. Zhong et al. analyze time expressions across formal and informal text and comprehensive and specific domain text [177, 178]. A line of research have devoted tremendous effort on time expression recognition and normalization in the clinical domain [12–14, 39, 54, 57, 67, 76, 84, 102, 103, 127, 138, 148, 150, 156, 170], in which the progress in clinical domain is mainly among the i2b2 challenge and the series of clinical TempEval shared tasks.

In SynTime and TOMN, we analyze time expressions in comprehensive and specific domains as well as in the formal and informal text [176–178].

2.1.3   Time Expression Type

2.1.3.1   TIMEX

In the concept of "time expression," the word "time" aims to restrict the task to those expressions involved in time information. The MUC-6 and MUC-7 [27, 28, 53] concern only two types of time expressions: DATE and TIME. DATE includes the complete or partial date expressions (e.g., "February 1975" and "third quarter of 1991") while TIME includes the complete or partial expressions of time of day (e.g., "5 p.m. EST" and "twelve o'clock noon"). The time expressions in text are annotated by the pair of markups <TIMEX> and </TIMEX>. Following examples show the annotation format for the two types of time expressions.

Example 2.1   <TIMEX TYPE="DATE">February 1975</TIMEX>

Example 2.2   <TIMEX TYPE="DATE">third quarter of 1991</TIMEX>

Example 2.3   <TIMEX TYPE="TIME">5 p.m. EST</TIMEX>

Example 2.4   <TIMEX TYPE="TIME">twelve o'clock noon</TIMEX>

2.1.3.2   TIMEX2

In the early of 2000s, Lisa Ferro and colleagues from MITRE Corporation extended the work of [27] to consider the meaning of time expressions by replacing the TYPE (i.e., DATE vs. TIME) categorization attribute with a set of attributes to represent the actual time indicated by the expressions [41–43, 98]. They use the pair of markups <TIMEX2> and </TIMEX2> with seven attributes (i.e., VAL, MOD, SET, COMMENT, PERIODICITY, GRANULARITY, and NON_SPECIFIC) to annotate the time expressions in text, in which VAL is the most important attribute whose value follows the ISO 8601 time standard. Following examples show the TIMEX2 annotation format.

Example 2.5 <TIMEX2 VAL="1999-08-03">two weeks</TIMEX2> from <TIMEX2 VAL="1999-07-20">next Tuesday</TIMEX2>

Example 2.6 I tutored an English student <TIMEX2 VAL="1998-WXX-4" SET="YES" GRANULARITY="G1D">some Thursdays</TIMEX2> in <TIMEX2 VAL="1999">1998</TIMEX2>.

Example 2.7 <TIMEX2 VAL="PT30M" MOD="LESS_THAN">almost half an hour</TIMEX2>

Example 2.8 <TIMEX2 VAL="1998-SU">Last summer</TIMEX2>, I went to the beach on <TIMEX2 VAL="1998-WXX-6" SET="YES" GRANULARITY="G1D">numerous Saturdays</TIMEX2>.

2.1.3.3 TIMEX3

In 2003, [120] introduced TimeML, a specification language that extends TIMEX and TIMEX2 to include both of time expressions and events and uses the pair of markups <TIMEX3> and </TIMEX3> to annotate the time expressions.[1] TIMEX3 includes four types of time expressions, namely DATE, TIME, SET, and DURATION, with value attribute (and some other attributes). SET includes the time expressions that express periodic times occurring with certain frequency (e.g., "every Monday" and "every quarter"). DURATION includes the time expressions that indicate intervening time between two time points of a time interval (e.g., "3 years" and "25 days"). Following shows some examples of the TIMEX3 annotation format.

Example 2.9 shot down the plane on <TIMEX3 tid="t1" type="DATE" value="1994-04-06" temporalFunction="false" functionInDocument="NONE"> April 6, 1994</TIMEX3>.

Example 2.10 A Brooklyn woman was killed <TIMEX3 tid="t2" type="TIME" value="1998-02-12TEV" temporalFunction="true" functionInDocument="NONE" anchorTimeID="t0">Thursday evening</TIMEX3> when . . .

Example 2.11 The official Iraqi News Agency gives the <TIMEX3 tid="t3" type="SET" value="XXXX-XX-XX">daily</TIMEX3> tally of inspections.

Example 2.12 In <TIMEX3 tid="t4" type="DURATION" value="PT1H" mod="LESS_THAN" temporalFunction="false" functionInDocument="NONE"> less than one hour</TIMEX3>

---

[1]Besides TIMEX3, TimeML also contains other three data structures: LINK, EVENT, and SIGNAL. This survey focuses on TIMEX3; for other three data structures, please refer to [120] for details.

Both TIMEX2 and TIMEX3 are developed as the annotation guidelines for creating normalized representations of time expressions (and their connection to events) in free text. Although they are complex and require much effort to master them well, they has been widely accepted as standards and extensively applied to the research related to time expressions in many languages.

2.1.3.4 Clinical TIMEX

Besides the four types of time expressions in the general domain (i.e., TIME, DATE, SET, DURATION), [12–14] defined two more types of time expressions for the analysis in the clinical domain: QUANTIFIER and PREPOSTEXP. QUANTIFIER includes the expressions that do not directly express time information but express the frequency that is constantly used in clinical domain, such as "twice" and "three times." PREPOSTEXP includes the time expressions in clinical domain that usually represents time points or spans relative to certain treatment or a clinical operation (e.g., "postoperatively").

2.1.4   TERN Evaluation

The shared tasks are essential for the progress of TERN development. In these shared tasks, many techniques are proposed to address the two tasks (i.e., time expression recognition and time expression normalization), such as TempEx [97], GUTime [161], HeidelTime [140], SUTime [24], ClearTK [10], and MedTime [84]. The equally important in these shared tasks are the evaluation metrics that are proposed to evaluate the systems. In the later development, these metrics become the standard criteria for the evaluation of TERN systems. In this section, we discuss the shared tasks and their evaluation metrics.

2.1.4.1 MUC Shared Tasks

In MUC-6 and MUC-7 events [27, 28, 53], the tasks of TERN are organized as part of the task of named entity recognition (NER), so the evaluation of TERN follows the one of NER. Specifically, a system is measured by two aspects: the ability to predict the exact span of the text and the ability to predict the type. A text span prediction is treated as correct if the text span is correct, regardless of the type prediction. A type prediction is treated as correct if the time expression is assigned with the correct type, regardless of text span. (The MUC shared tasks use the TIMEX, with only two types of time expressions, namely TIME and DATE.) For both of the text span and type predictions, three measures are involved: the number of ground-truth answers, the number of system predictions, and the number of possible time expressions in the systems. The three measures lead to two standard metrics: Precision and Recall.

$$Precision = \frac{N_{correct}}{N_{correct} + N_{incorrect}} \tag{2.1}$$

$$Recall = \frac{N_{correct}}{N_{key}} \tag{2.2}$$

where $N_{correct}$ denotes the number of correct predictions while $N_{incorrect}$ denotes the number of incorrect predictions; N_{key} denotes the total ground-truth time expressions.

The MUC shared tasks also use the micro-averaged F-measure (MAF) to represent the final score, which is the harmonic mean of precision and recall that is calculated over all the time expressions on both the aspects of text span and type. The F-measure tends to privilege the balanced systems.

2.1.4.2 ACE Shared Tasks

The ACE shared task has a complex procedure to evaluate the systems under a complex evaluation metrics. The ACE evaluation includes 9 metrics; besides the standard Precision, Recall, and F-measure that are similar to the MUC shared tasks and defined by Eqs. (2.1) and (2.2), ACE also includes the following 6 metrics: (a) CORR, the number of correct predictions, (b) INCO, the number of incorrect predictions, (c) MISS, the number of time expressions that a system is missing to predict, (d) SPUR, the number of predictions that are not in the ground-truth, (e) POSS, the sum of CORR, INCO, and MISS, and (f) ACT, the sum of CORR, INCO, and SPUR.

2.1.4.3 TempEval Shared Tasks

The TempEval shared tasks aim to automatically identify all the time expressions, events, and temporal relations within a text. In this survey, we focus on the time expressions. (The TempEval-2 use the TIMEX2 scheme while the TempEval-3 use the TIMEX3 scheme.) They use the three standard metrics to evaluate the performance of time expression recognition: Precision, Recall, and F_1; and uses the Accuracy to evaluate the performance of attribute classification and value normalization; the four metrics are defined by Eqs. (2.3), (2.4), (2.5), and (2.6).

$$Precision = \frac{TP}{TP + FP} \tag{2.3}$$

$$Recall = \frac{TP}{TP + FN} \tag{2.4}$$

$$F_1 = \frac{2 \times Precision \times Recall}{Precision + Recall} \qquad (2.5)$$

$$Accuracy = \frac{Number \; of \; correct \; answers}{Number \; of \; total \; answers} \qquad (2.6)$$

where TP is the number of time expressions that are in both of system predictions and ground-truth, FP is the number of time expressions that are in the system predictions but not in the ground-truth, and FN is the number of time expressions that are in the ground-truth but not in the system predictions.

The three standard metrics are measured under two kinds of matches, namely strict match and relaxed match. The strict match indicates the exact match between the time expressions that a system is predicting and the ground-truth time expressions, while the relaxed match indicates the overlap between the predicted time expressions and the ground-truth time expressions.

2.1.4.4 Clinical TempEval Shared Tasks

The clinical TempEval shared tasks bring the tasks of temporal information extraction to the clinical domain. The first three clinical TempEval shared tasks (i.e., 2015, 2016, and 2017) include a variety of tasks covering the time expression recognition and normalization [12–14], while the 2018 clinical TempEval shared task mainly concerns the task of parsing time expression normalization [76]. The clinical TempEval shared tasks concern six types of time expressions, with two more addition to the four types in the general TempEval shared tasks, as illustrated in Sect. 2.1.3.4. For the evaluation, the clinical TempEval shared tasks follow the general TempEval shared tasks to use the standard metrics of Precision, Recall, and F_1, as defined in Eqs. (2.3), (2.4), and (2.5).

2.1.5 Time Expression Recognition

Although most approaches address the problem of time expression recognition together with time expression normalization as an end-to-end task, we discuss the two sub-tasks separately so as to better understand each of them. This section focuses on the time expression recognition and next section discuss the time expression normalization.

The methods for time expression recognition are mainly categorized into two kinds: rule-based methods and learning-based methods.

Rule-Based Methods Rule-based time taggers like TempEx, GUTime, HeidelTime, and SUTime mainly predefine a set of time-related words and regular expression patterns [24, 97, 140, 161]. HeidelTime hand-crafts rules with time resources like weekdays, seasons, and months, and leverages language clues like part-of-speech (POS) to identify time expression and then normalize them to the standard form in a pipeline UIMA (Unstructured Information Management Architecture[2]) [140]. SUTime [24] designs deterministic rules using a cascade finite automata [62] on regular expressions over tokens [25]. It firstly identifies individual words, then expands them to chunks, and finally to the full time expressions. Other rule-based taggers include FSS-TimEx [175], which uses finite-state rule cascades to recognize time expressions. These rule-based time taggers achieve very good performance in the TempEval shared tasks. Specifically, HeidelTime achieves the highest F_1 of 86% in TempEval-2 [163] and SUTime achieves the highest F_1 of 91.3% under the relaxed match in the TempEval-3 [159]. In the clinical evaluations (including the i2b2 challenge and clinical TempEval shared tasks) [12, 13, 148], the top systems develop corresponding rules based on either HeidelTime or SUTime to recognize the time expressions from clinical text.

Naturally, our SynTime is also a rule-based time expression tagger, while the key differences between SynTime and other rule-based taggers are that between the rules and the specific tokens SynTime introduces a layer of token type, and the rules that SynTime designs work on the token types, and are independent of specific tokens [178]. Moreover, the rules are designed in a heuristic way, leading SynTime to be much more flexible and expansible. As we will see, SynTime achieves much better results on various datasets in comparison with both rule-based taggers and learning-based taggers.

Learning-Based Methods Machine learning-based methods mainly extract features from text and apply statistical models on these features for recognizing time expressions. Those features include character features (e.g., the first and last 3 characters of a word), word features (e.g., current, previous, and subsequent words), syntactic features (e.g., part-of-speech and noun phrase chunks), semantic features (e.g., lexical semantics and semantic role), and gazetteer features (e.g., matching in a dictionary) [10, 44, 45, 89]. Those statistical models include Markov logic network, logistic regression, support vector machines, maximum entropy, and conditional random fields [10, 45, 69, 89, 158]. These methods mainly leverage information from labeled data under supervised learning. Some of learning-based methods achieve good performance, and even the highest F_1 of 82.71% under strict match in TempEval-3 [10].

Outside the TempEval shared tasks, Angeli et al. leverage compositional grammar and employ an EM-style approach to learn a latent parser for time expression recognition [5]. In the method UWTime, Lee et al. employ a combinatory categorial grammar (CCG) [139] to define a set of lexicon with rules and use L1-regularization to learn from linguistic context for time expression recognition [78]. These two methods explicitly use linguistic information. In UWTime, especially, CCG could capture rich structure information of language, similar to the rule-based methods.

---

[2]http://uima.apache.org.

Tabassum et al. focus on resolving the dates in tweets, and use distant supervision to recognize time expressions [155]. With the development of neural networks and deep learning, Some researchers use variants of neural networks and word embeddings to represent and recognize time expressions [40, 72, 83].

Unlike those methods that use standard features [10, 44, 45, 55, 69, 89, 158], TOMN derives only a kind of pre-tag features and lemma features according to the characteristics of time expressions, which can enhance the impact of significant features and reduce the impact of insignificant features [177]. Unlike those methods that use fixed structure information [4, 5, 78], TOMN uses loose structure information by grouping the constituent words of time expression under three main token types, which can fully account for the loose structure of time expressions. More importantly, TOMN models time expressions under a CRFs framework with a constituent-based tagging scheme, which can keep tag assignment consistent.

2.1.6 Time Expression Normalization

Those methods that are developed for time expression normalization in the TempEval shared tasks and clinical evaluations (e.g., i2b2 challenge and clinical TempEval shared tasks) are mainly based on rules [10, 12, 13, 45, 89, 97, 140, 148, 158, 161]. Because these rule systems share high similarity, Llorens et al. suggest to construct a large public knowledge base for the normalization task [90]. Some researchers treat the normalization problem as a learning task; Lee et al. [78] use AdaGrad algorithm and Tabassum et al. [155] use a log-linear algorithm to normalize time expressions. Recently, Berhard and Parker [11] and Laparra et al. [75] develop a semantically compositional annotation scheme to specify time expressions by which they can leverage machine learning techniques for this normalization task.

SynTime and TOMN focus on time expression recognition and leave the task of time expression normalization to those highly similar rule-based methods or to the future work.

2.2 Named Entity Recognition and Classification

The research on named entity recognition and classification has a long history. Nadeau and Sekine [109] review its development of early years (from 1991 to 2006) in terms of languages (e.g., English, German, and Chinese) [26, 27, 53, 128, 164], text genres (e.g., scientific and journalistic) and domains (e.g., sports and business) [99, 104, 117], entity categories (e.g., PERSON, LOCATION, ORGANIZATION, and MISC) [27, 47, 53, 79, 128], learning methods (e.g., supervised, semi-supervised, and unsupervised learnings) [15, 20, 33, 110, 133], statistical learning techniques (e.g., hidden Markov models, maximum entropy models, and conditional random fields) [6, 15, 18, 101, 133], engineering features (e.g., word-level features, dictionary features, and document and corpus features) [15, 32, 33, 124, 136, 174], and shared task evaluations (e.g., ACE, MUC, and CoNLL) [27, 38, 53, 128].

Before the era of deep learning and neural networks, there are also works that consider several aspects of NERC, like leveraging unlabeled data for NERC [81], leveraging external knowledge for NERC [29, 71, 123], nested NERC [1, 46], and NERC in informal text [88, 126].

In the era of deep learning and neural networks, researchers employ neural networks and word embeddings to develop variants of models on the CoNLL03, ACE2004, and OntoNotes NERC dataset [29, 34, 37, 63, 74, 85, 87, 92, 93, 115, 116, 129, 146].

UGTO benefits some features (i.e., basic word and lemma features and general POS tags) from these traditional methods, and refines significant features (i.e., uncommon words and proper nouns) according to an in-depth analysis for the characteristics of named entities. Unlike these neural network-based methods that mainly compute semantic similarities among words, UGTO focuses on the distinction between named entities and common text. And unlike most NERC methods that treat named entity recognition and classification as an end-to-end joint task, we focus on named entity recognition and demonstrates that joint modeling of named entity recognition and classification does not improve the performance of named entity recognition [176, 179, 180].

2.2.1   Named Entity Classification

A line of research is concerned with the problem of NEC (also known as entity typing), which assumes that named entities are already recognized from text. A variety of techniques have been developed for this problem [33, 48, 51, 86, 94, 111, 114, 125, 173]. These research leverage many features similar to the ones derived for the end-to-end NERC, such as bag of words, POS tags, and n-gram strings. A key difference between NEC and NERC is that researchers do not formulate NEC as a problem of sequence tagging but treat a whole named entity as a unit. We focus on NER and leave NEC to future work.

2.3   Syntactic Parsing and Semantic Parsing

There have been considerable efforts trying to jointly model syntactic parsing and semantic parsing under an optimization framework which aims to simultaneously resolve these two parsings in the same time. However, almost all these efforts waste but justify that those attempts that try to jointly model syntactic and semantic parsings will fail in the end. Sutton and McCallum [152] report that their approach for joint syntactic parsing and semantic role labeling gets negative results. In the CoNLL2008 and CoNLL2009 shared tasks on the joint syntactic and semantic parsings, those systems that perform the best are those ones that develop separate syntactic models and semantic models [56, 151]. Specifically, [68] achieve the best results in the CoNLL2008 shared task by developing separate models; they report that their joint model fails to improve the performance over their separate models. In subsequent research, a series of techniques are employed to develop joint models for syntactic and semantic parsings on the CoNLL2008 and CoNLL2009 datasets, but none of them can further improve the performance in comparison with those best separate models [61, 91, 135, 153]. Hashimoto et al. [58] jointly model many linguistic tasks, including syntactic tasks and semantic tasks; among their experiments, the joint modeling of multiple syntactic and semantic tasks fails to improve the performance compared with those individual tasks. The most possible reason of these failure is that in theory, syntax and semantics lie at different levels of linguistic analyses, as shown in Fig. 6.4 [30, 31, 70, 105, 106]; in practice, the joint modeling of syntactic and semantic tasks requires a trade-off between these two linguistic tasks, and in that trade-off these two linguistic tasks will hurt each other in terms of their performance.

A line of research, which is slightly related to our work, is concerned about the necessity and usefulness of syntactic parsing for semantic analysis [50, 118, 119, 154]. These empirical results demonstrate that syntactic parsing can significantly improve the performance of semantic analysis, but the premise is that syntactic parsing is finished before semantic parsing starts. These results are consistent with the syntactic and semantic theories [30, 31, 70, 105, 106] as well as the layout of the syntactic-semantic structure, as shown in Fig. 6.4.

References

1. Alex B, Haddow B, Grover C (2007) Recognising nested named entities in biomedical text. In: Proceedings of the workshop on BioNLP 2007: biological, translational, and clinical language processing, p 65–72
2. Alonso O, Strotgen J, Baeza-Yates R, Gertz M (2011) Temporal information retrieval: challenges and opportunities. In: Proceedings of 1st international temporal web analytics workshop, p 1–8
3. Altuna B, Aranzabe MJ, de Ilarraza AD (2017) Eusheideltime: time expression extraction and normalisation for basque. Procesamiento del Lenguaje Natural 59:15–22
4. Angeli G, Uszkoreit J (2013) Language-independent discriminative parsing of temporal expressions. In: Proceedings of the 51st annual meeting of the association for computational linguistics, p 83–92
5. Angeli G, Manning CD, Jurafsky D (2012) Parsing time: learning to interpret time expressions. In: Proceedings of 2012 conference of the north american chapter of the association for computational linguistics: human language technologies, p 446–455
6. Asahara M, Matsumoto Y (2003) Japanese named entity extraction with redundant morphological analysis. In: Proceedings of the 2003 Conference of the North American chapter of the association for computational linguistics on human language technology, p 8–15
7. de Azevedo RF, Joao Pedro Santos Rodrigues MRdSR, Moro CMC (2018) Temporal tagging of noisy clinical texts in brazilian. In: Proceedings of international conference on computational processing of the Portuguese language, p 231–241

8. Baldwin JA (2002) Learning temporal annotation of French news. Master's thesis, Graduate School of Arts and Sciences, Georgetown University
9. Berglund A (2004) Extracting temporal information and ordering events for Swedish. Master's thesis
10. Bethard S (2013) Cleartk-timeml: a minimalist approach to tempeval 2013. In: Proceedings of the 7th international workshop on semantic evaluation, p 10–14
11. Bethard S, Parker JL (2016) A semantically compositional annotation scheme for time normalization. In: Proceedings of the 2016 conference on language resources and evaluation, p 3779–3786
12. Bethard S, Derczynski L, Savova G, Pustejovsky J, Verhagen M (2015) Semeval-2015 task 6: clinical tempeval. In: Proceedings of the 9th international workshop on semantic evaluation, p 806–814
13. Bethard S, Savova G, Chen WT, Derczynski L, Pustejovsky J, Verhagen M (2016) Semeval-2016 task 12: clinical tempeval. In: Proceedings of the 10th international workshop on semantic evaluation, p 1052–1062
14. Bethard S, Savova G, Palmer M, Pustejovsky J (2017) Semeval-2017 task 12: clinical tempeval. In: Proceedings of the 11th international workshop on semantic evaluation, p 565–572
15. Bikel DM, Miller SL, Schwartz RM, Weischedel RM (1997) Nymble: a high-performance learning name-finder. In: Proceedings of the fifth conference on applied natural language processing, p 194–201
16. Bittar A, Amsili P, Denis P, Danlos L (2011) French timebank: an ISO-TimeML annotated reference corpus. In: Proceedings of the 49th annual meeting of the association for computational linguistics, p 130–134
17. Boguraev B, Pustejovsky J, Ando R, Verhagen M (2007) Timebank evolution as a community resource for TimeML parsing. Lang Resour Eval 41(1):91–115
18. Borthwick A, Sterling J, Agichtein E, Grishman R (1998) NYU: description of the MENE named entity system as used in MUC-7. In: Proceedings of the 7th message understanding conference
19. Boudaa T, Marouani ME, Enneya N (2018) Arabic temporal expression tagging and normalization. In: Proceedings of international conference on big data, cloud and applications, p 546–557
20. Brin S (1998) Extracting patterns and relations from the world wide web. In: Proceedings of the international workshop on the world wide web and databases, p 172–183
21. van de Camp M, Christiansen H (2012) Resolving relative time expressions in Dutch text with constraint handling rules. In: Proceedings of the 7th international workshop on constraint solving and language processing, pp 74–85
22. Campos R, Dias G, Jorge AM, Jatowt A (2014) Survey of temporal information retrieval and related applications. ACM Comput Surv 47(2):15:1–41
23. Caselli T, Lenzi VB, Sprugnoli R, Pianta E, Prodanof I (2011) Annotating events, temporal expressions and relations in Italian: the It-TimeML experience for the Ita-TimeBank. In: Proceedings of the 5th linguistic annotation workshop, p 143–151
24. Chang AX, Manning CD (2012) Sutime: a library for recognizing and normalizing time expressions. In: Proceedings of 8th international conference on language resources and evaluation, p 3735–3740
25. Chang AX, Manning CD (2014) Tokensregex: defining cascaded regular expressions over tokens. Tech. rep., Department of Computer Science, Stanford University
26. Chen HH, Lee JC (1996) Identification and classification of proper nouns in Chinese texts. In: Proceedings of the 16th conference on computational linguistics, p 222–229
27. Chinchor NA (1998) MUC-7 named entity task definition. In: Proceedings of the 7th message understanding conference, vol 29
28. Chinchor NA (1998) Overview of MUC-7/MET-2. In: Proceedings of the 7th message understanding conference

29. Chiu JP, Nichols E (2016) Named entity recognition with bidirectional LSTM-CNNs. Trans Assoc Comput Linguist 4:357–370
30. Chomsky N (1957) Syntactic structures. Mouton Publishers, Berlin
31. Chomsky N (1965) Aspects of the theory of syntax. MIT Press, Cambridge
32. Collins M (2002) Ranking algorithms for named-entity extraction: boosting and the voted perceptron. In: Proceedings of the 40th annual meeting on association for computational linguistics, p 489–496
33. Collins M, Singer Y (1999) Unsupervised models for named entity classification. In: Proceedings of the 1999 joint SIGDAT conference on empirical methods in natural language processing and very large corpora
34. Collobert R, Weston J, Bottou L, Karlen M, Kavukcuoglu K, Kuksa PP (2011) Natural language processing (almost) from scratch. J Mach Learn Res 12:2493–2537
35. Costa F, Branco A (2012) Timebankpt: a timeml annotated corpus of Portuguese. In: Proceedings of the 8th international conference on language resources and evaluation, p 3727–3734
36. Degaetano-Ortlieb S, Strötgen J (2017) Diachronic variation of temporal expressions in scientific writing through the lens of relative entropy. In: Proceedings of international conference of the German society for computational linguistics and language technology, p 259–275
37. Devlin J, Chang MW, Lee K, Toutanova K (2019) Bert: pre-training of deep bidirectional transformers for language understanding. In: Proceedings of the 2019 conference of the North American chapter of the association for computational linguistics: human language technologies, association for computational linguistics, Minneapolis, Minnesota, vol 1, p 4171–4186
38. Doddington G, Mitchell A, Przybocki M, Ramshaw L, Strassel S, Weischedel R (2004) The automatic content extraction (ACE) program tasks, data, and evaluation. In: Proceedings of the 2004 conference on language resources and evaluation, p 1–4
39. D'Souza J, Ng V (2013) Classifying temporal relations in clinical data: a hybrid, knowledge-rich approach. J Biomed Inform 46:S29–S39
40. Etcheverry M, Wonsever D (2017) Time expressions recognition with word vectors and neural networks. In: Proceedings of the 24th international symposium on temporal representation and reasoning, p 1–12
41. Ferro L (2001) Tides instruction manual for the annotation of temporal expressions. Tech. rep., MITRE
42. Ferro L, Mani I, Sundheim B, Wilson G (2001) Tides temporal annotation guidelines—version 1.0.2. Tech. rep., MITRE
43. Ferro L, Gerber L, Mani I, Sundheim B, Wilson G (2005) Tides 2005 standard for the annotation of temporal expressions. Tech. rep., MITRE
44. Filannino M, Nenadic G (2015) Temporal expression extraction with extensive feature type selection and a posteriori label adjustment. Data Knowl Eng 100:19–23
45. Filannino M, Brown G, Nenadic G (2013) Mantime: temporal expression identification and normalization in the TempEval-3 challenge. In: Proceedings of the 7th international workshop on semantic evaluation, p 53–57
46. Finkel JR, Manning C (2009) Nested named entity recognition. In: Proceedings of the 2009 conference on empirical methods in natural language processing, p 141–150
47. Fleischman M (2001) Automated subcategorization of named entities. In: Proceedings of the student research workshop and tutorial abstracts, ACL (companion volume), p 25–30
48. Fleischman M, Hovy E (2002) Fine grained classification of named entities. In: Proceedings of the 19th international conference on Computational linguistics, p 1–7
49. Forascu C, Tufis D (2012) Romanian timebank: an annotated parallel corpus for temporal information. In: Proceedings of the 8th international conference on language resources and evaluation, p 3762–3766

50. Gildea D, Palmer M (2002) The necessity of parsing for predicate argument recognition. In: Proceedings of the 40th annual meeting on association for computational linguistics, p 239–246
51. Giuliano C (2009) Fine-grained classification of named entities exploiting latent semantic kernels. In: CoNLL
52. Grabar N, Hamon T (2018) Automatic detection of temporal information in Ukrainian general-language texts. Tech. rep., CNRS University Lille and LIMSI University Paris-Saclay
53. Grishman R, Sundheim B (1996) Message understanding conference—6: a brief history. In: Proceedings of the 16th international conference on computational linguistics
54. Grouin C, Grabar N, Hamon T, Rosset S, Tannier X, Zweigenbaum P (2013) Eventual situations for timeline extraction from clinical reports. J Am Med Inform Assoc 20:820–827
55. Hacioglu K, Chen Y, Douglas B (2005) Automatic time expression labeling for English and Chinese text. In: Proceedings of the 6th international conference on intelligent text processing and computational linguistics, p 548–559
56. Hajič J, Ciaramita M, Johansson R, Kawahara D, Martí MA, Màrquez L, Meyers A, Nivre J, Padó S, Štěpánek P, Surdeanu M, Xue N, Zhang Y (2009) The CoNLL-2009 shared task: syntactic and semantic dependencies in multiple languages. In: Proceedings of the 13th conference on computational natural language learning, p 1–18
57. Hao T, Pan X, Gu Z, Qu Y, Weng H (2018) A pattern learning-based method for temporal expression extraction and normalization from multi-lingual heterogeneous clinical texts. BMC Med Inform Decis Making 18:16–25
58. Hashimoto K, Xiong C, Tsuruoka Y, Socher R (2017) A joint many-task model: growing a neural network for multiple NLP tasks. In: Proceedings of the 2017 conference on empirical methods in natural language processing, p 1923–1933
59. He R, Qin B, Liu T, Pan Y, Li S (2008) A novel heuristic error-driven learning for recognizing Chinese time expression. J Chin Lang Comput 18(4):139–159
60. He RF, Qin B, Liu T, Pan YQ, Li S (2007) Recognizing the extent of Chinese time expressions based on the dependency parsing and error-driven learning. J Chin Inform Process 21(5):36–40
61. Henderson J, Merlo P, Titov I, Musillo G (2013) Multilingual joint parsing of syntactic and semantic dependencies with a latent variable model. Comput Linguist 39(4):949–998
62. Hobbs JR, Appelt DE, Bear J, Israel D, Kameyama M, Stickel M, Tyson M (1997) Fastus: a cascaded finite-state transducer for extracting information from natural-language text. In: Finite state devices for natural language processing, p 383–406
63. Huang Z, Xu W, Yu K (2015) Bidirectional LSTM-CRF models for sequence tagging. https://arxiv.org/abs/1508.01991v1
64. Im S, You H, Jang H, Nam S, Shin H (2009) Ktimeml: specification of temporal and event expressions in Korean text. In: Proceedings of the 7th workshop on asian language resources, ACL-IJCNLP 2009, p 115–122
65. Jang SB, Baldwin J, Mani I (2004) Automatic timex2 tagging of Korean news. ACM Trans Asian Lang Inform Process 3(1):51–65
66. Jeong YS, Joo WT, Do HW, Lim CG, Choi KS, Choi HJ (2016) Korean timeml and Korean timebank. In: Proceedings of the tenth international conference on language resources and evaluation, p 356–359
67. Jindal P, Roth D (2013) Extraction of events and temporal expressions from clinical narratives. J Biomed Inform 46:S13–S19
68. Johansson R, Nugues P (2008) Dependency-based syntactic-semantic analysis with Propbank and Nombank. In: Proceedings of the 12th conference on computational natural language learning, p 183–187
69. Jung H, Stent A (2013) Att1: temporal annotation using big windows and rich syntactic and semantic features. In: Proceedings of the 7th international workshop on semantic evaluation, pp 20–24
70. Katz JJ, Fodor JA (1963) The structure of a semantic theory. Language 39(2):170–210

71. Kazama J, Torisawa K (2007) Exploiting Wikipedia as external knowledge for named entity recognition. In: Proceedings of the 2007 joint conference on empirical methods in natural language processing and computational natural language learning, p 698–707
72. Kim ZM, Jeong YS (2016) Timex3 and event extraction using recurrent neural networks. In: Proceedings of the 2016 IEEE international conference on big data and smart computing, p 450–453
73. Kolomiyets O, Moens MF (2009) Meeting TempEval-2: shallow approach for temporal tagger. In: Proceedings of the NAACL HLT workshop on semantic evaluation: recent achievements and future directions, p 52–57
74. Lample G, Ballesteros M, Subramanian S, Kawakami K, Dyer C (2016) Neural architecture for named entity recognition. In: Proceedings of the 15th annual conference of the North American chapter of the association for computational linguistics, p 260–270
75. Laparra E, Xu D, Bethard S (2018) From characters to time intervals: new paradigms for evaluation and neural parsing of time normalizations. Trans Assoc Comput Linguist 6:343–356
76. Laparra E, Xu D, Bethard S, Elsayed AS, Palmer M (2018) Semeval 2018 task 6: parsing time normalizations. In: Proceedings of the 12th international workshop on semantic evaluation, p 88–96
77. Lavelli A, Magnini B, Negri M, Pianta E, Speranza M, Sprugnoli R (2005) Italian content annotation bank (I-CAB): temporal expressions (v. 1.0). Tech. rep., ITC-irst, Centro per la Ricerca Scientifica e Technologica Povo
78. Lee K, Artzi Y, Dodge J, Zettlemoyer L (2014) Context-dependent semantic parsing for time expressions. In: Proceedings of the 52th annual meeting of the association for computational linguistics, p 1437–1447
79. Lee S, Lee GG (2005) Heuristic methods for reducing errors of geographic named entities learned by bootstrapping. In: Proceedings of the international conference on natural language processing, p 658–669
80. Li H, Strötgen J, Zell J, Gertz M (2014) Chinese temporal tagging with heideltime. In: Proceedings of the 14th conference of the European chapter of the association for computational linguistics, p 133–137
81. Liang P (2005) Semi-supervised learning for natural language. Master's thesis, Massachusetts Institute of Technology
82. Lim CG, Choi HJ (2017) Efficient temporal information extraction from Korean documents. In: Proceedings of IEEE 18th international conference on mobile data management, p 366370
83. Lin C, Miller T, Dligach D, Bethard S, Savova G (2017) Representations of time expressions for temporal relation extraction with convolutional neural networks. In: Proceedings of the 16th workshop on biomedical natural language processing, p 322–327
84. Lin YK, Chen H, Brown RA (2013) Medtime: a temporal information extraction system for clinical narratives. J Biomed Inform 46:S20–S28
85. Ling W, Dyer C, Black AW, Trancoso I, Fermandez R, Amir S, Marujo L, Luis T (2015) Finding function in form: compositional character models for open vocabulary word representation. In: Proceedings of the 2015 conference on empirical methods in natural language processing, p 1520–1530
86. Ling X, Weld DS (2012) Fine-grained entity recognition. In: Proceedings of the twenty-sixth conference on artificial intelligence
87. Liu L, Shang J, Ren X, Xu FF, Gui H, Peng J, Han J (2018) Empower sequence labeling with task-aware neural language model. In: Proceedings of the 32nd AAAI conference on artificial intelligence
88. Liu X, Zhang S, Wei F, Zhou M (2011) Recognizing named entities in tweets. In: Proceedings of the 49th annual meeting of the association for computational linguistics, p 359–367
89. Llorens H, Saquete E, Navarro B (2010) Tipsem (English and Spanish): evaluating CRFs and semantic roles in TempEval-2. In: Proceedings of the 5th international workshop on semantic evaluation, p 284–291

90. Llorens H, Derczynski L, Gaizauskas R, Saquete E (2012) Timen: an open temporal expression normalisation resource. In: Proceedings of the 8th international conference on language resources and evaluation, p 3044–3051
91. Lluís X, Carreras X, Màrquez L (2013) Joint arc-factored parsing of syntactic and semantic dependencies. Trans Assoc Comput Linguist 1:219–230
92. Luo G, Huang X, Lin CY, Nie Z (2015) Joint named entity recognition and disambiguation. In: Proceedings of the 2005 conference on empirical methods in natural language processing, p 879–888
93. Ma X, Hovy E (2016) End-to-end sequence labeling via bi-directional LSTM-CNNs-CRF. In: Proceedings of the 54th annual meeting of the association for computational linguistics (volume 1: long papers), p 1064–1074
94. Ma Y, Cambria E, Gao S (2016) Label embedding for zero-shot fine-grained named entity typing. In: Proceedings of the 26th international conference on computational linguistics, p 171–180
95. Manfredi G, Strötgen J, Zell J, Gertz M (2014) Heideltime at eventi: tuning Italian resources and addressing timeml's empty tags. In: Proceedings of the 4th international workshop EVALITA, p 39–43
96. Mani I (2003) Recent developments in temporal information. In: Proceedings of the international conference on recent advances in natural language processing, p 45–60
97. Mani I, Wilson G (2000) Robust temporal processing of news. In: Proceedings of the 38th annual meeting on Association for Computational Linguistics, p 69–76
98. Mani I, Wilson G, Ferro L, Sundheim B (2001) Guidelines for annotation temporal information. In: Proceedings of the first international conference on human language technology research, p 1–3
99. Maynard D, Tablan V, Ursu C, Cunningham H, Wilks Y (2001) Named entity recognition from diverse text types. In: Proceedings of 2001 recent advances in natural language processing conference, p 257–274
100. Mazur P, Dale R (2010) Wikiwars: a new corpus for research on temporal expressions. In: Proceedings of the 2010 conference on empirical methods in natural language processing, p 913–922
101. McCallum A, Li W (2003) Early results for named entity recognition with conditional random fields, feature induction and web-enhanced lexicons. In: Proceedings of the 7th conference on computational natural language learning
102. Miller T, Bethard S, Dligach D, Pradhan S, Lin C, Savova G (2013) Discovering narrative containers in clinical text. In: Proceedings of the 2013 workshop on biomedical natural language processing, p 18–26
103. Miller T, Bethard S, Dligach D, Lin C, Savova G (2015) Extracting time expressions from clinical text. In: Proceedings of the 2015 workshop on biomedical natural language processing, p 81–91
104. Minkov E, Wang RC, Cohen WW (2005) Extracting personal names from email: applying named entity recognition to informal text. In: Proceedings of the conference on human language technology and empirical methods in natural language processing, p 443–450
105. Montague R (1970) Universal grammar. Theoria 36:373–398
106. Montague R (1973) The proper treatment of quantification in ordinary English. In: Approaches to natural language, p 221–242
107. Moriceau V, Tannier X (2014) French resources for extraction and normalizationg of temporal expressions with heideltime. In: Proceedings of the 9th international conference on language resources and evaluation, p 3239–3243
108. Murat A, Yusup A, Iskandar Z, Yusup A, Abaydulla Y (2018) Applying lexical semantics to automatic extraction of temporal expressions in Uyghur. J Inform Process Syst 14(4):824–836
109. Nadeau D, Sekine S (2007) A survey of named entity recognition and classification. Lingvisticae Investigationes 30(1):3–26

110. Nadeau D, Turney PD, Matwin S (2006) Unsupervised named-entity recognition: generating gazetteers and resolving ambiguity. In: Proceedings of the Conference of the Canadian society for computational studies of intelligence, p 266–277
111. Nakashole N, Tylenda T, Weikum G (2013) Fine-grained semantic typing of emerging entities. In: Proceedings of the 51st annual meeting of the association for computational linguistics, p 1488–1497
112. Negri M, Marseglia L (2004) Recognition and normalization of time expressions: ITC-IRST at tern 2004. Tech. rep., ITC-IRST
113. Negri M, Saquete E, Martinez-Barco P, Munoz R (2006) Evaluating knowledge-based approaches to the multilingual extension of a temporal expression normalizer. In: Proceedings of the workshop on annotating and reasoning about time and events, p 30–37
114. Niu C, Li W, Ding J, Srihari RK (2003) A bootstrapping approach to named entity classification using successive learners. In: Proceedings of the 41st annual meeting on association for computational linguistics, vol 1, p 335–342
115. Passos A, Kumar V, McCallum A (2014) Lexicon infused phrase embeddings for named entity resolution. In: Proceedings of the 8th conference on computational language learning, p 78–86
116. Peters ME, Ammar W, Bhagavatula C, Power R (2017) Semi-supervised sequence tagging with bidirectional language models. In: Proceedings of the 55th annual meeting of the association for computational linguistics, p 1756–1765
117. Poibeau T, Kosseim L (2001) Proper name extraction from non-journalistic texts. Lang Comput 37:144–157
118. Punyakanok V, Roth D, tau Yih W (2005) The necessity of syntactic parsing for semantic role labeling. In: Proceedings of the 19th international joint conference on artificial intelligence, p 1117–1123
119. Punyakanok V, Roth D, Yih WT (2007) The importance of syntactic parsing and inference in semantic role labeling. Comput Linguist 6(9):1–30
120. Pustejovsky J, Castano J, Ingria R, Sauri R, Gaizauskas R, Setzer A, Katz G, Radev D (2003) Timeml: robust specification of event and temporal expressions in text. New Dir Quest Answering 3:28–34
121. Pustejovsky J, Hanks P, Sauri R, See A, Gaizauskas R, Setzer A, Sundheim B, Radev D, Day D, Ferro L, Lazo M (2003) The timebank corpus. Corpus Linguist 2003:647–656
122. Pustejovsky J, Lee K, Bunt H, Romary L (2010) ISO-TimeML: an international standard for semantic annotation. In: Proceedings of the seventh conference on international language resources and evaluation (LREC'10), p 394–397
123. Ratinov L, Roth D (2009) Design challenges and misconceptions in named entity recognition. In: Proceedings of the thirteenth conference on computational natural language learning, p 147–155
124. Ravin Y, Wacholder N (1997) Extracting names from natural-language text. Tech. rep., IBM Research Division
125. Ren X, He W, Qu M, Huang L, Ji H, Han J (2016) Afet: automatic fine-grained entity typing by hierarchical partial-label embedding. In: Proceedings of the 2016 conference on empirical methods in natural language processing, p 1369–1378
126. Ritter A, Clark S, Mausam, Etzioni O (2011) Named entity recognition in tweets: an experimental study. In: Proceedings of the 2011 conference on empirical methods in natural language processing, p 1524–1534
127. Roberts K, Rink B, Harabagiu SM (2013) A flexible framework for recognizing events, temporal expressions, and temporal relations in clinical text. J Am Med Inform Assoc 20(5):867–875
128. Sang EFTK, Meulder FD (2003) Introduction to the CoNLL-2003 shared task: language-independent named entity recognition. In: Proceedings of the 7th conference on natural language learning, pp 142–147
129. Santos CND, Guimaraes V (2015) Boosting named entity recognition with neural character embeddings. In: Proceedings of the 5th named entities workshop, p 25–33

130. Saquete E, Martinez-Barco P, Munoz R (2002) Recognizing and tagging temporal expressions in Spanish. In: Proceedings of LREC workshop on annotation standards for temporal information in natural language, p 44–51
131. Saquete E, Martinez-Barco P, Munoz R (2004) Evaluation of the automatic multilinguality for time expression resolution. In: Proceedings of the 15th international workshop on database and expert systems applications, p 25–30
132. Sauri R, Saquete E, Pustejovsky J (2010) Annotating time expressions in Spanish TimeML annotation guidelines (version TempEval-2010). Tech. rep., Barcelona Media - Innovation Center
133. Sekine S (1998) Nyu: description of the Japanese ne system used for met-2. In: Proceedings of the 7th message understanding conference
134. Setzer A, Gaizauskas R (2000) Annotating events and temporal information in newswire texts. In: Proceedings of the second international conference on language resources and evaluation, p 1287–1294
135. Shi P, Zhang Y (2017) Joint bi-affine parsing and semantic role labeling. In: Proceedings of the 2017 international conference on asian language processing, p 338–341
136. Silva JFD, Kozareva Z, Lopes JGP (2004) Cluster analysis and classification of named entities. In: Proceedings of the 2004 conference on language resources and evaluation
137. Skukan L, Glavas G, Snajder J (2014) Heideltime.hr: extracting and normalizing temporal expressions in croatian. In: Proceedings of the 9th Slovenian language technologies conference, p 99–103
138. Sohn S, Wagholikar KB, Li D, Jonnalagadda SR, Tao C, Elayavilli RK, Liu H (2013) Comprehensive temporal information detection from clinical text: medical events, time, and tlink identification. J Am Med Inform Assoc 20(5):836–842
139. Steedman M (1996) Surface structure and interpretation. The MIT Press, Cambridge
140. Strötgen J, Gertz M (2010) Heideltime: high quality rule-based extraction and normalization of temporal expressions. In: Proceedings of the 5th international workshop on semantic evaluation (SemEval'10). Association for Computational Linguistics, Stroudsburg, p 321–324
141. Strötgen J, Gertz M (2011) Wikiwarsde: a German corpus of narratives annotated with temporal expressions. In: Proceedings of German Society for computational linguistics and language technology, p 129–134
142. Strötgen J, Gertz M (2012) Temporal tagging on different domains: challenges, strategies, and gold standards. In: Proceedings of 8th international conference on language resources and evaluation, p 3746–3753
143. Strotgen J, Gertz M (2013) Multilingual and cross-domain temporal tagging. Lang Resour Eval 47(2):269–198
144. Strötgen J, Zell J, Gertz M (2013) Heideltime: tuning English and developing Spanish resources. In: Proceedings of the second joint conference on lexical and computational semantics (SEM), p 15–19
145. Strötgen J, Armiti A, Canh TV, Zell J, Gertz M (2014) Time for more languages: temporal tagging of Arabic, Italian, Spanish, and Vietnamese. ACM Trans Asian Lang Inform Process 13(1):1–21
146. Strubell E, Verga P, Belanger D, McCallum A (2017) Fast and accurate entity recognition with iterated dilated convolutions. In: Proceedings of the 2017 conference on empirical methods in natural language processing, p 2670–2680
147. Styler IV WF, Bethard S, Finan S, Palmer M, Pradhan S, De Groen PC, Erickson B, Miller T, Lin C, Savova G, Pustejovsky J (2014) Temporal annotation in the clinical domain. Trans Assoc Comput Linguist 2:143–154
148. Sun W, Rumshisky A, Uzuner O (2013) Annotating temporal information in clinical narratives. J Biomed Inform 46:S5–S12
149. Sun W, Rumshisky A, Uzuner O (2013) Evaluating temporal relations in clinical text: 2012 i2b2 challenge. J Am Med Inform Assoc 20:806–813

150. Sun W, Rumshisky A, Uzuner O (2015) Normalization of relative and incomplete temporal expressions in clinical narratives. J Am Med Inform Assoc 22(5):1001–1008
151. Surdeanu M, Johansson R, Meyers A, Màrquez L, Nivre J (2008) The CoNLL-2008 shared task on joint parsing of syntactic and semantic dependencies. In: Proceedings of the 12th conference on computational natural language learning, p 159–177
152. Sutton C, McCallum A (2005) Joint parsing and semantic role labeling. In: Proceedings of the 9th conference on computational natural language learning, p 225–229
153. Swayamdipta S, Ballesteros M, Dyer C, Smith NA (2016) Greedy, joint syntactic-semantic parsing with stack LSTMs. In: Proceedings of the 20th SIGNLL conference on computational natural language learning, p 187–197
154. Swayamdipta S, Thomson S, Lee K, Zettlemoyer L, Dyer C, Smith NA (2018) Syntactic scaffolds for semantic structures. In: Proceedings of the 2018 conference on empirical methods in natural language processing, p 3772–3782
155. Tabassum J, Ritter A, Xu W (2016) Tweetime: a minimally supervised method for recognizing and normalizing time expressions in twitter. In: Proceedings of the 2016 conference on empirical methods in natural language processing, p 307–318
156. Tang B, Wu Y, Jiang M, Chen Y, Denny JC, Xu H (2013) A hybrid system for temporal information extraction from clinical text. J Am Med Inform Assoc 20:828–835
157. Taule M, Marti T, Recasens M (2008) Ancora: multilevel annotated corpora for catalan and Spanish. In: Proceedings of the 6th international conference on language resources and evaluation
158. UzZaman N, Allen JF (2010) Trips and trios system for TempEval-2: extracting temporal information from text. In: Proceedings of the 5th international workshop on semantic evaluation, p 276–283
159. UzZaman N, Llorens H, Derczynski L, Verhagen M, Allen J, Pustejovsky J (2013) Semeval-2013 task 1: TempEval-3: evaluating time expressions, events, and temporal relations. In: Proceedings of the 7th international workshop on semantic evaluation, p 1–9
160. Vazov N (2001) A system for extraction of temporal expressions from French texts based on syntactic and semantic constraints. In: Proceedings of the workshop on temporal and spatial information processing, p 14–21
161. Verhagen M, Mani I, Sauri R, Knippen R, Jang SB, Littman J, Rumshisky A, Phillips J, Pustejovsky J (2005) Automating temporal annotation with TARQI. In: Proceedings of the ACL interactive poster and demonstration sessions, p 81–84
162. Verhagen M, Gaizauskas R, Schilder F, Hepple M, Katz G, Pustejovsky J (2007) Semeval-2007 task 15: tempeval temporal relation identification. In: Proceedings of the 4th international workshop on semantic evaluation, p 75–80
163. Verhagen M, Sauri R, Caselli T, Pustejovsky J (2010) Semeval-2010 task 13: TempEval-2. In: Proceedings of the 5th international workshop on semantic evaluation, p 57–62
164. Wang LJ, Li WC, Chang CH (1992) Recognizing unregistered names for mandarin word identification. In: Proceedings of the 14th conference on computational linguistics, vol 4, p 1239–1243
165. Wilson G, Mani I, Sundheim B, Ferro L (2001) A multilingual approach to annotating and extracting temporal information. In: Proceedings of the workshop on temporal and spatial information processing, p 12
166. Wong KF, Xia Y, Li W, Yuan C (2005) An overview of temporal information extraction. International J Comput Process Orient Lang 18(2):137–152
167. Wu M, Li W, Chen Q, Lu Q (2005) Normalizing Chinese temporal expressions with multi-label classification. In: Proceedings of the 2th international conference on natural language processing and knowledge engineering, p 318–323
168. Wu M, Li W, Lu Q, Li B (2005) Ctemp: a Chinese temporal parser for extracting and normalizing temporal information. In: Proceedings of the second international joint conference on natural language processing, p 694–706
169. Wu T, Zhou Y, Huang X, Wu L (2010) Chinese time expression recognition based on automatically generated basic-time-unit rules. J Chin Inform Process 24(4):3–10

170. Xu Y, Wang Y, Liu T, Tsujii J, Chang EIC (2013) An end-to-end system to identify temporal relation in discharge summaries: 2012 i2b2 challenge. J Am Med Inform Assoc 20:849–858
171. Yadav V, Bethard S (2018) A survey on recent advances in named entity recognition from deep learning models. In: Proceedings of the 27th international conference on computational linguistics, p 2145–2158
172. Yin B, Jin B (2017) A multi-label classification method on Chinese temporal expressions based on character embedding. In: Proceedings of the 4th international conference on information science and control engineering, p 51–54
173. Yogatama D, Gillick D, Lazic N (2015) Embedding methods for fine grained entity type classification. In: Proceedings of the 53rd annual meeting of the association for computational linguistics and the 7th international joint conference on natural language processing (vol 2: short papers), vol 2, p 291–296
174. Yu S, Bai S, Wu PS (1998) Description of the Kent ridge digital labs system used for MUC-7. In: Proceedings of the 7th message understanding conference
175. Zavarella V, Tanev H (2013) Fss-timex for TempEval-3: extracting temporal information from text. In: Proceedings of the 7th international workshop on semantic evaluation, p 58–63
176. Zhong X (2020) Time expression and named entity analysis and recognition. PhD thesis, Nanyang Technological University, Singapore
177. Zhong X, Cambria E (2018) Time expression recognition using a constituent-based tagging scheme. In: Proceedings of the 2018 world wide web conference, Lyon, p 983–992
178. Zhong X, Sun A, Cambria E (2017) Time expression analysis and recognition using syntactic token types and general heuristic rules. In: Proceedings of the 55th annual meeting of the association for computational linguistics, Vancouver, vol 1, p 420–429
179. Zhong X, Cambria E, Hussain A (2020) Extracting time expressions and named entities with constituent-based tagging schemes. Cogn Comput 12(4):844–862
180. Zhong X, Cambria E, Hussain A (2021) Does semantics aid syntax? An empirical study on named entity recognition and classification. Neural Comput Appl

Chapter 3
Data Analysis

Abstract We analyze four diverse datasets about time expressions for their intrinsic characteristics and find five such common characteristics; similarly we analyze two well-known benchmark datasets about named entities for their intrinsic characteristics and find three such common characteristics. For the common characteristics of time expressions, firstly, most time expressions are very short, consisting of about 2 words on average; secondly, most time expressions contain at least one time-related word that can distinguish time expressions from common text; thirdly, only a small group of words are used to express time information; fourthly, words in time expressions demonstrate similar syntactic behaviour; and finally, time expressions are formed by loose structure, with more than 53.5% of time tokens appearing in different positions within time expressions. For the common characteristics of named entities, firstly, most named entities contain uncommon words, which mainly appear in named entities and hardly appear in common text; secondly, named entities are mainly made up of proper nouns, with more than 84.8% of proper nouns appear in named entities under the whole text and more than 80.1% of the words are proper nouns within named entities; thirdly, named entities are formed by loose structure, with more than 53.77% of distinct words that appear in different positions within named entities.

Keywords Short time expressions · Time token · Loose structure · Proper nouns · Small group of time words

In this chapter, we detail our analysis for the intrinsic characteristics of time expressions from four diverse datasets and for the ones of named entities from two benchmark datasets. According to the analysis we summarize such five common characteristics about time expressions and two common characteristics about named entities [11–14].

3.1   Time Expression Analysis

3.1.1   Time Expression Datasets

We conduct an analysis on the following four diverse datasets: TimeBank, TE3-Silver, WikiWars, and Tweets. TimeBank [6] is a benchmark dataset in the series of the TempEval competitions [8–10], and it consists of 183 news articles. TE3-Silver is a large-scale dataset with 2452 news articles that are collected from the Gigaword corpus [4]; its time expressions are automatically labeled by other three time taggers (i.e., TIPSem and and it is constructed as a silver dataset in the TempEval-3 competition [8]. The WikiWars dataset is constructed by collecting articles about some famous wars from Wikipedia [3]. Tweets is our manually labeled dataset that consists of 942 tweets, of which each contains one or more time expressions [13].

Specifically, the Tweets dataset is constructed through the following procedure. We randomly sample 4000 tweets and apply SUTime on these tweets, among which 942 tweets contain at least one time expression that identified by SUTime. From the remaining 3058 tweets, we randomly sample 500 and manually annotate them, finding that only 15 tweets contain time expressions. Therefore, we roughly consider that SUTime misses about 3% time expressions in tweets. Two annotators then manually annotate these 942 tweets with discussion to a final agreement according to the standards of TimeML and TimeBank. Finally, we obtain 1127 manually labeled time expressions. For these 942 tweets, we randomly sample 200 tweets as the test set, and the remaining 742 as the training set.

Table 3.1 summarizes the statistics of these four datasets.

3.1.2   Time Expression Characteristics

Although these four datasets are diverse from each other in terms of sources, corpus sizes, text types, and domains, we will see that their time expressions demonstrate some similar characteristics. From our analysis, we find five such common characteristics about time expressions.

Characteristic 1 *Time expressions are very short, consisting of about 2 words on average.*

Table 3.1 Statistics of the four datasets. A tweet here is viewed as a document

Dataset	# documents	# words	# timexes
TimeBank	183	61,418	1243
TE3-Silver	2452	666,309	12,739
WikiWars	22	119,468	2671
Tweets	942	18,199	1127

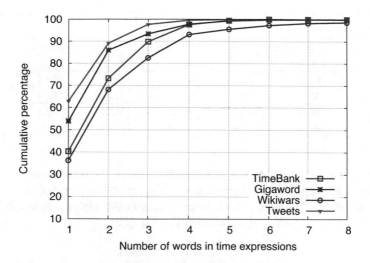

Fig. 3.1 Length distributions of time expressions in the four analyzed datasets

Table 3.2 Average length of time expressions in these four datasets

Dataset	Average length
TimeBank	2.00
TE3-Silver	1.70
WikiWars	2.38
Tweets	1.51

Figure 3.1 plots the distributions of the length of time expressions in the four analyzed datasets.[1] Although these four datasets are other in terms of sources (e.g., news articles, Wikipedia articles, and tweets) and corpus sizes (e.g., the numbers of words range from 18,199 to 666,309), the length of their time expressions follows a similar distribution. Most time expressions are very short, with more than 80% of time expressions containing no more than three words and more than 90% containing no more than four words. In particular, the percentages of one-word time expressions range from 36.23% in WikiWars through 40.31% in TimeBank and 53.85% in TE3-Silver to 62.91% in Tweets. This indicates that in informal communication, people tend to use words in minimal length to express time information. Table 3.2 presents the average length of time expressions in each dataset. On average, a typical time expression contains about two words.

Characteristic 2 *Most time expressions contain time token(s). Time tokens can distinguish time expressions from common text while modifiers and numerals cannot.*

---

[1]The length distribution of time expressions is the original inspiration when I discover that power-law distributions widely appear in the length-frequency of entities from different types of entities and different languages [1, 16].

Table 3.3 Percentage of the three kinds of constituent words of time expressions that appear in time expressions (P_{timex}) and in common text (P_{text})

Dataset	Time token		Modifier		Numeral	
	P_{timex}	P_{text}	P_{timex}	P_{text}	P_{timex}	P_{text}
TimeBank	94.61	0.34	47.39	22.56	22.61	3.16
TE3-Silver	96.44	0.65	28.05	22.82	20.24	2.03
WikiWars	91.81	0.14	31.64	26.14	38.01	9.82
Tweets	96.01	0.50	21.38	13.03	18.81	1.28

Table 3.3 presents the percentage of the three kinds of constituent words of time expressions that appear in time expressions (P_{timex}) and in common text (P_{text}). Here "common text" includes the whole text with time expressions excluded. P_{timex} is defined by Eq. (3.1) while P_{text} is defined by Eq. (3.2),

$$P_{timex}(T) = \frac{\#timex\ that\ contain\ T}{\#total\ timex} \tag{3.1}$$

$$P_{text}(T) = \frac{\#tokens\ that\ are\ T}{\#total\ tokens} \tag{3.2}$$

where $T \in \{time\ token,\ modifier,\ numeral\}$.

The second column of Table 3.3 shows that most time expressions contain time tokens, with more than 91.8% of time expressions containing at least one time-related token. Some time expressions without time token depend on other time expressions. In the sequence "95–100 days," for example, the time expression "95" depends on the time expression "100 days." By contrast, the third column shows that no more than 0.7% of common text contain time tokens. This indicates that time tokens can distinguish time expressions from common text. On the other hand, the last four columns demonstrate that on average, 32.1% of time expressions and 21.1% of common text contain modifiers, and 24.9% of time expressions and 4.1% of common text contain numerals. This indicates that modifiers and numerals cannot distinguish time expressions from common text.

Looking at the Tweets dataset, we can find that the P_{timex} of time tokens (96.0%) is relatively high while the P_{timex} of modifiers (21.4%) and numerals (18.8%) are much lower than the ones of other datasets. This suggests that in Twitter people tend to use time expressions with fewer modifiers and numerals.

Characteristic 3 *Only a small group of time words are used to express time information.*

From our analysis on the time expressions in these four datasets, we find that the group of words used to express time information is small.

Table 3.4 presents the number of distinct words and of distinct time tokens. "Distinct" here means ignoring the word variants and frequencies during counting. Words (or tokens) are manually normalized before counting and their variants are

Table 3.4 Number of distinct words and distinct time tokens in time expressions

Dataset	No. of words	No. of time tokens
TimeBank	130	64
TE3-Silver	214	80
WikiWars	224	74
Tweets	107	64

ignored. For example, "month," "months," and "mths" are treated the same as "month" and are counted only once; similarly, "year" and "5yrs" are counted as the same token "year." Numerals in the counting are ignored. As shown in Table 3.4, although these four datasets vary in sizes, domains, and text types, the numbers of their distinct time tokens are comparable and their sizes are small, with only about 70 (distinct time tokens). That means time expressions highly overlap at their time tokens within an individual dataset.

Across these four datasets, the number of distinct words is 350, which is about half of the simple summation, 675; the number of distinct time tokens in total is 123, less than half of the simple summation, 282. Among the 123 distinct time tokens, 45 appear in all these four datasets, and 101 appear in at least two datasets. This indicates that time tokens, which account for time expressions, are highly overlapped across the four datasets. In other words, time expressions highly overlap at their time tokens.

Characteristic 4 *POS tags cannot distinguish time expressions from common words, but within time expressions, POS tags can distinguish their constituents.*

Table 3.5 lists the top 10 most frequent POS tags that appear in time expressions, and their percentages over the corresponding tags in the whole text, defined by Eq. (3.3)

$$Perc(t) = \frac{number\ of\ t\ in\ time\ expressions}{number\ of\ t\ in\ the\ whole\ text} \tag{3.3}$$

where t denotes a POS tag.

Note that the Tweets dataset includes only those 942 manually annotated tweets that contain at least one time expression; if taking into account those tweets that do not contain time expressions (which are 3058 tweets; see Sect. 4.4.1), the $Perc$ of the POS tags in Tweets will be much lower. Among these 40 POS tags (10 × 4 datasets), 36 have the $Perc$ lower than 20%; other 4 POS tags are 3 CD and 1 RB. For each of the TimeBank, TE3-Silver, and WikiWars datasets, except the CD, all the POS tags have the $Perc$ less than 10%. This indicates that POS tags cannot provide enough information to distinguish time expressions from common words. However, the most common POS tags in time expressions are NN*, JJ, RB, CD, and DT. Within time expressions, time tokens usually have NN* and RB, modifiers have JJ and RB, and numerals have CD. This finding indicates that for time expressions, their similar constituent words behave in a similar syntactic way. When seeing this, I realize that this is exactly how linguists define part-of-speech

Table 3.5 Top 10 most frequent POS tags that appear in time expressions and their percentages over the corresponding tags in the whole text. *Freq* denotes the number of times a POS tag appearing in time expressions while *Perc* denotes the percentage of this POS tag in time expressions over the corresponding tag in the whole dataset

TimeBank			TE3-Silver			WikiWars			Tweets		
Tag	Freq	Percent	Tag	Freq	Percent	Tag	Freq	Percent	Tag	Freq	Percent
NN	587	6.66	NNP	6902	8.77	CD	2113	67.85	NN	572	15.27
DT	396	7.16	CD	4582	22.11	NNP	1294	8.87	CD	323	55.40
CD	351	11.60	NN	3233	3.26	NN	783	5.70	RB	189	25.40
JJ	347	8.74	DT	2080	3.15	DT	582	4.67	DT	161	18.05
NNP	336	5.09	JJ	1940	3.82	IN	363	2.48	NNP	155	6.55
NNS	156	4.17	NNS	1356	3.19	JJ	328	3.82	JJ	118	12.38
RB	162	9.44	RB	597	3.52	RB	261	8.23	NNS	116	18.10
IN	76	1.13	IN	512	0.62	NNS	234	3.82	IN	20	1.24
,	20	0.61	,	175	0.56	,	171	2.80	JJR	10	17.86
CC	9	0.60	CC	69	0.38	VBG	28	1.50	VBP	9	2.72

for language; "linguists group some words of language into classes (sets) which show similar syntactic behaviour" [2]. **This is my eureka moment!** The definition of part-of-speech for language inspires us to define a syntactic type system for the time expression that is part of language (see Sect. 4.1 for our defined syntactic type system).

Characteristic 5 *Time expressions are formed by loose structure, with more than 53.5% of time tokens appearing in different positions within time expressions.*

We find that time expressions are formed by loose structure and the loose structure mainly exhibits in the following two aspects. Firstly, many time expressions consist of loose collocations. For example, the time token "September" can form a time expression by itself, or forms "September 2006" by another time token appearing after it, or forms "1 September 2006" by a numeral appearing before it and another time token appearing after it. Secondly, some time expressions can change their word order without changing their meanings. For example, "September 2006" can be written as "2006 September" with the same meaning. From the point of view of the positions within time expressions, the time token "September" may appear as the (i) beginning or (ii) inside word of a time expression when time expressions are modeled by the BIO scheme; or it may appear as (1) a unit-word time expression, or the (2) beginning, (3) inside, (4) last word of a multi-word time expression when time expressions are modeled by the BILOU scheme.

Table 3.6 presents the percentages of distinct time tokens and distinct modifiers that appear in different positions within time expressions. "Different positions" here means the two different positions under the BIO scheme and at least two of the four different positions under the BILOU scheme. For each dataset, under the BIO scheme, more than 53.5% of distinct time tokens appear in different positions, and under the BILOU scheme, more than 61.4% of distinct time tokens appear

Table 3.6 Percentage of distinct time tokens and distinct modifiers that appear in different positions within time expressions

Dataset	BIO scheme		BILOU scheme	
	Time token	Modifier	Time token	Modifier
TimeBank	58.18	33.33	63.64	33.33
TE3-Silver	61.29	45.83	77.05	46.00
WikiWars	53.57	26.19	61.40	29.55
Tweets	67.21	27.59	72.58	27.59

in different positions. The number of modifiers that appear in different positions is more than 27.5%. When the BIO scheme or the BILOU scheme is used to model time expressions, the appearance in different positions leads to inconsistent tag assignment, and the inconsistent tag assignment causes difficulty for statistical models to model time expressions. We need to explore an appropriate tagging scheme (see Sect. 5.1 for details).

The first four characteristics are related to the principle of least effort [17]. That is, people tend to act with least effort so as to minimize the cost of energy at both individual and collective levels in all the human actions, including language use [17]. Time expressions are part of language and act as an interface of communication. Short expressions, occurrence and distinction, small vocabulary, and similar syntactic behaviour all reduce the cost of energy required for our humans to communicate with each other. The last characteristic demonstrates that the structure of time expressions is flexible.

To summarize: on average, a typical time expression contains two words, among which one is a time token and the other is a modifier or numeral, and the number of total distinct time tokens is small. Therefore, in order to recognize a time expression, we first recognize its time token, then recognize its modifier or numeral.

3.2 Named Entity Analysis

3.2.1 Named Entity Datasets

We conduct an analysis on the following two benchmark datasets for the characteristics of named entities: CoNLL03 and OntoNotes*. The original CoNLL03 and OntoNotes5 copora include the data in English and other languages for named entity analysis and other tasks, but here we focus our analysis on named entity analysis in the English data.

CoNLL03 is a small benchmark dataset that is derived from the Reuters RCV1 corpus, with 1393 news articles collected between August 1996 and August 1997. This dataset contains 4 entity categories: PER, LOC, ORG, and MISC [7].

OntoNotes* is a dataset that is derived from the large-scale benchmark OntoNotes5 dataset [5]. OntoNotes5 is a portion of the OnteNotes 5.0 corpus for named entity analysis and consists of 3370 articles that are collected from different

Table 3.7 Statistics of the two datasets. "Whole" indicates the whole dataset

Dataset	Portion	# documents	# words	# entities	# categories
CoNLL03	Training set	946	203,621	23,499	4
	Development set	216	51,362	5942	
	Test set	231	46,435	5648	
	Whole	**1393**	**301,418**	**35,089**	
OntoNotes*	Training set	2729	1,578,195	81,222	11
	Development set	406	246,009	12,721	
	Test set	235	155,330	7537	
	Whole	**3370**	**1,979,534**	**101,480**	

sources (e.g., broadcast, newswire, weblogs, and telephone conversation) over a long period of time. It includes 18 entity categories.[2] Although the OntoNotes5 dataset is a benchmark dataset, we find that its annotation is far from perfect. For example, its guideline "OntoNotes Named Entity Guidelines (Version 14.0)" states that the **ORDINAL** includes all the ordinal numbers and the **CARDINAL** includes the whole numbers, fractions, and decimals, but we find in the common text 3588 numeral words, which is 7.1% of the total numeral words. In addition, some sequences are annotated inconsistently. For the sequence "the Cold War," for example, in some cases the whole sequence is annotated as a named entity (i.e., "**<ENAMEX>**the Cold War**</ENAMEX>**," where "**ENAMEX**" is the annotation mark) while in some other cases only "Cold War" is annotated as a named entity (i.e., "the **<ENAMEX>**Cold War**</ENAMEX>**").

To get a high-quality dataset for named entity analysis, we derive a dataset termed OntoNotes* from the OntoNotes5 dataset by (1) removing those entity categories whose named entities are mainly composed of numbers and ordinals[3] and (2) moving all the "the" at the beginning of named entities and all the "'s" at the end of named entities outside their named entities (e.g., all the "**<ENAMEX>**the Cold War 's**</ENAMEX>**" are changed to "the **<ENAMEX>**Cold War**</ENAMEX>** 's").

When setting training, development, and test sets, we follow the setting by the CoNLL03 shared task [7] for the CoNLL03 dataset and follow the setting[4] by one of OntoNotes5's authors for our OntoNotes* dataset. Table 3.7 summarizes the statistics of these two datasets.

---

[2]The 18 entity categories in the OntoNotes5 dataset are **CARDINAL, DATE, EVENT, FAC, GPE, LANGUAGE, LAW, LOC, MONEY, NORP, ORDINAL, ORG, PERCENT, PERSON, PRODUCT, QUANTITY, TIME,** and **WORK_OF_ART.**

[3]The removed entity categories include **CARDINAL, DATE, MONEY, ORDINAL, PERCENT, QUANTITY,** and **TIME.**

[4]https://github.com/ontonotes/conll-formatted-ontonotes-5.0.

Table 3.8 Percentage of named entities that contain at least one word hardly appearing in the common text

	Whole	Training set	Development set	Test set
CoNLL03	97.77	98.77	99.19	98.62
OntoNotes*	92.91	92.20	95.22	95.61

3.2.2 Named Entity Characteristics

Like the above four datasets used to analyze time expressions, these two benchmark datasets are different from each other in terms of corpus size, text genre, and entity categories, but we will see soon that their named entities demonstrate some similar characteristics.

Characteristic 6 *Most named entities contain uncommon word(s), with more than 92.2% of named entities having at least one word that hardly appears in common text.*

Table 3.8 presents the percentages of named entities that contain at least one word hardly appearing in common text (case sensitive). Here "common text" includes the whole text with named entities excluded. The percentage is calculated within a set that contains named entities and common text, and the set can be a whole dataset (e.g., the CoNLL03 dataset) or only a splitting set (e.g., the training set of the CoNLL03 dataset). Within a set, for a word w, the rate of its occurrences in named entities over its occurrences in the whole text is defined by Eq. (3.4):

$$r(w) = \frac{f_{entity}(w)}{f_{entity}(w) + f_{common}(w)} \tag{3.4}$$

where $f_{entity}(w)$ denotes the occurrences of w in named entities while $f_{common}(w)$ denotes the occurrences of w in common text. If $r(w)$ reaches a threshold R, then the word w is treated as hardly appearing in common text. For the CoNLL03 dataset and its splitting sets, R is set by 1, which means that the word does not appear in common text. For the OntoNotes* dataset and its splitting sets, R is set by 0.95, because its annotation is imperfect (as mentioned in Sect. 3.2.1): its common text contains some words that should be treated as named entities, such as "American."[5] We call such kind of words that mainly appear in named entities and hardly appear in common text *uncommon words*.

From Table 3.8 we can see that for a set, more than 92.2% of named entities contain at least one uncommon word. This phenomenon of uncommon words widely exists in the CoNLL03 and OntoNotes* datasets and their training sets, development sets, and test sets. An implication of this phenomenon is that for a dataset, the

---

[5]The threshold $R = 0.95$ for the OntoNotes* dataset is an empirical value. We think that the imperfect annotation should be controlled to an acceptable degree.

Table 3.9 Top 4 most frequent POS tags in named entities and their percentage over the whole tags within named entities (p_{entity}) and over the corresponding tags in the whole text (p_{whole})

CoNLL03			OntoNotes*		
POS	P_{entity}	P_{whole}	POS	P_{entity}	P_{whole}
NNP	83.81	84.82	NNP	77.67	85.88
JJ	5.82	17.57	JJ	4.60	6.77
NN	4.89	6.46	NN	4.57	2.91
NNPS	1.55	94.12	NNPS	2.50	93.04

uncommon words of its development and test sets also hardly appear in the common text of its training set. This suggests that these words of its test set that hardly appear in the common text of its training set tend to predict named entities.

Characteristic 7 *Named entities are mainly made up of proper nouns. In the whole text, more than 84.8% of proper nouns appear in named entities; within named entities, more than 80.1% of the words are proper nouns.*

We find that named entities are mainly made up of proper nouns.[6] Table 3.9 lists the top 4 most frequent POS tags appearing in named entities and their percentages over the whole POS tags in named entities (p_{entity}) and over the corresponding POS tags in the whole text (p_{whole}). p_{entity} is defined by Eq. (3.5) and p_{whole} is defined by Eq. (3.6).

$$p_{entity}(t) = \frac{f_{entity}(t)}{\sum_{t_i} f_{entity}(t_i)} \qquad (3.5)$$

$$p_{whole}(t) = \frac{f_{entity}(t)}{f_{entity}(t) + f_{common}(t)} \qquad (3.6)$$

where t denotes a POS tag, $f_{entity}(t)$ denotes the occurrences of the tag t in named entities while $f_{common}(t)$ denotes the occurrences of the tag t in common text.

From Table 3.9 we can see that the top 4 POS tags in both the CoNLL03 and OntoNotes* datasets are the same and they are **NNP**, **JJ**, **NN**, and **NNPS**. The p_{entity} of proper nouns (including **NNP** and **NNPS**) reaches more than 80.1%, and this indicates that named entities are mainly made up of proper nouns. The p_{whole} of proper nouns reaches more than 84.8%, and this indicates that in the whole text,

---

[6]If we take into account the original OntoNotes5 dataset, then these named entities are mainly made up of proper nouns and cardinal numbers.

Table 3.10 Percentage of distinct words that appear in different positions within named entities

Dataset	BIO scheme	BILOU scheme
CoNLL03	53.77	59.14
OntoNotes*	57.13	79.67

the proper nouns mainly appear in named entities.[7] Within named entities, these JJ words are mainly the nationality words, such as "American" and "Chinese."

Characteristic 8 *Named entities are formed by loose structure, with more than 53.77% of distinct words that appear in different positions within named entities.*

We find that named entities are also formed by loose structure, similar to time expressions (see Characteristic 5). Table 3.10 presents the percentages of distinct words that appear in different positions within time expression.[8] The definition of "different positions" is same as the one defined in Sect. 3.1.2. From Table 3.10 we can see that for each dataset, under the BIO scheme, more than 53.77% of distinct words appear in different positions, and under the BILOU scheme, more than 59.14% of distinct words appear in different positions. The appearance of words in different positions within named entities causes the position-based tagging scheme to suffer from the problem of inconsistent tag assignment, and we need to another appropriate tagging scheme (see Sect. 6.1.3 for details).

References

1. Estoup JB (1916) Gammes stenographiques. In: Institut Stenographique de France, Paris
2. Manning C, Schutze H (1999) Foundations of statistical natural language processing. MIT Press, Cambridge
3. Mazur P, Dale R (2010) Wikiwars: a new corpus for research on temporal expressions. In: Proceedings of the 2010 conference on empirical methods in natural language processing, p 913–922
4. Parker R, Graff D, Kong J, Chen K, Maeda K (2011) English gigaword, 5th edn
5. Pradhan S, Moschitti A, Xue N, Ng HT, Bjorkelund A, Uryupina O, Zhang Y, Zhong Z (2013) Towards robust linguistic analysis using ontonotes. In: Proceedings of the 7th conference on computational natural language learning, p 143–152
6. Pustejovsky J, Hanks P, Sauri R, See A, Gaizauskas R, Setzer A, Sundheim B, Radev D, Day D, Ferro L, Lazo M (2003) The timebank corpus. Corpus Linguist 2003:647–656

---

[7]The P_{text} of proper nouns does not reach 100% mainly because an individual dataset concerns certain types of named entities and partly because some NNP* words are incorrectly POS tagged, for example, "SURPRISE DEFEAT" is wrongly tagged as "NNP NNP," but it should be tagged as "JJ NN."

[8]We here do not report the percentages of different positions of different constituent words of named entities but simply report the ones of distinct words, due to two reasons: firstly, the vocabulary of named entities is large and it is difficult to collect all of them; secondly, the percentage of the different positions of distinct words is enough to reflect the loose structure of named entities.

7. Sang EFTK, Meulder FD (2003) Introduction to the CoNLL-2003 shared task: language-independent named entity recognition. In: Proceedings of the 7th conference on natural language learning, p 142–147
8. UzZaman N, Llorens H, Derczynski L, Verhagen M, Allen J, Pustejovsky J (2013) Semeval-2013 task 1: TempEval-3: Evaluating time expressions, events, and temporal relations. In: Proceedings of the 7th international workshop on semantic evaluation, p 1–9
9. Verhagen M, Gaizauskas R, Schilder F, Hepple M, Katz G, Pustejovsky J (2007) Semeval-2007 task 15: tempeval temporal relation identification. In: Proceedings of the 4th international workshop on semantic evaluation, p 75–80
10. Verhagen M, Sauri R, Caselli T, Pustejovsky J (2010) Semeval-2010 task 13: TempEval-2. In: Proceedings of the 5th international workshop on semantic evaluation, p 57–62
11. Zhong X (2020) Time expression and named entity analysis and recognition. PhD thesis, Nanyang Technological University, Singapore
12. Zhong X, Cambria E (2018) Time expression recognition using a constituent-based tagging scheme. In: Proceedings of the 2018 world wide web conference, Lyon, p 983–992
13. Zhong X, Sun A, Cambria E (2017) Time expression analysis and recognition using syntactic token types and general heuristic rules. In: Proceedings of the 55th annual meeting of the association for computational linguistics, Vancouver, vol 1, p 420–429
14. Zhong X, Cambria E, Hussain A (2020) Extracting time expressions and named entities with constituent-based tagging schemes. Cogn Comput 12(4):844–862
15. Zhong X, Cambria E, Rajapakse JC (2021) Power-law distributions in length-frequency of entities. In: submission to the joint conference of the 59th annual meeting of the association for computational linguistics and the 11th international joint conference on natural language processing
16. Zipf G (1936) The Psychobiology of language. Routledge, London
17. Zipf G (1949) Human behavior and the principle of least effort: an introduction to human ecology. Addison-Wesley, Readings

Chapter 4
SynTime: Token Types and Heuristic Rules

Abstract According to the five common characteristics of time expressions, we propose a type-based approach named SynTime for time expression recognition. Specifically, we define three main syntactic token types, namely *time token*, *modifier*, and *numeral*, to group time-related token regular expressions. On the types we design general heuristic rules to recognize time expressions. In recognition, SynTime first identifies time tokens from raw text, then searches their surroundings for modifiers and numerals to form time segments, and finally merges the time segments to time expressions. As a light-weight rule-based tagger, SynTime runs in real time, and can be easily expanded by simply adding keywords for the text from different domains and different text types. Evaluation on benchmark datasets and tweets data shows that SynTime outperforms state-of-the-art methods.

Keywords Time token · Token types · Heuristic rules · Type-based tagger

SynTime defines a syntactic token-type system for the constituent words of time expressions, and designs a small set of heuristic rules working on these token types [12, 13]. Figure 1.1a shows the layout of SynTime, which mainly consists of three levels: token level, type level, and rule level. At the token level, there lie specific tokens and token regular expressions. At the type level, token types group these tokens and token regular expressions. At the rule level, heuristic rules work on token types and are independent of specific tokens. For example, heuristic rules do not work on the tokens "1989" and "February," but work on their token types "YEAR" and "MONTH." In other words, our heuristic rules are designed in a general manner. For this reason, our token types and heuristic rules are independent of specific domains, specific text types, and even specific languages that consist of specific tokens. In this book, we test SynTime on specific domains (i.e., general

Fig. 4.1 Overview of
SynTime in practice. The
left-hand side shows the
SynTime construction, with
an initialization using token
regular expressions and an
optional expansion using the
training text. The right-hand
side shows the three main
steps of how SynTime
recognizes time expressions

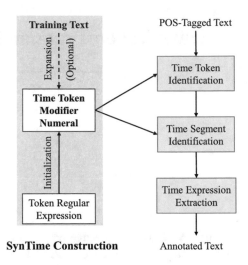

domain and war domain) and specific text types (i.e., formal text and informal text)
in English. Testing on other languages needs to construct a set of token regular
expressions in the target languages under our defined token-type system or another
defined token-type system.

Figure 4.1 displays the overview of SynTime in practice. As shown on the left-
hand side, SynTime is initialized with token regular expressions. After initialization,
SynTime can be directly applied on text to recognize time expressions. On the
other hand, SynTime can be easily expanded by simply adding time-related token
regular expressions derived from training text under these defined token types. The
expansion enables SynTime to recognize time expressions from the text in different
domains and different textual types.

As shown on the right-hand side of Fig. 4.1, SynTime recognizes time expressions from unstructured text through three main steps. In the first step, SynTime
identifies time tokens from the POS-tagged raw text. Around these identified
time tokens, in the second step, SynTime searches for modifiers and numerals to
form time segments. In the last step, SynTime transforms time segments to time
expressions.

4.1 SynTime Construction

We define a syntactic token-type system for the constituent words of time expressions, specifically, 15 token types are defined for time tokens, 5 token types are for
modifiers, and 1 token type for numerals. These token types are described below

Table 4.1 SynTime defines 15 token types for time tokens, 5 token types for modifiers, and 1 token type for numerals. The last column indicates the number of distinct tokens that are grouped under the token type, without counting token variants. "–" indicates that the token type involves changing digits and cannot be counted

Token type	Description	Examples	No. of tokens
Time token			
DECADE	Decade instances	1910s, 1940s, fifties	–
YEAR	Year instances	1970, 1989, 2006	–
SEASON	Season instances	Summer, Winter	5
MONTH	Month instances	February, September	12
WEEK	Day of the week	Monday, Friday	7
DATE	Date instances	2016-09-07, 9/2006	–
TIME	Time instances	03:45:32, 20:43	–
DAY_TIME	Time within a day	Morning, afternoon	27
TIMELINE	Relative to today	Yesterday, tomorrow	12
HOLIDAY	Holiday instances	Christmas	20
PERIOD	Period instances	Daily	9
DURATION	Duration instances	5-year	–
TIME_UNIT	Time units	Year(s)	15
TIME_ZONE	Time zones	GMT, UTC	6
ERA	Era AD and BC	AD, BC	2
Modifier			
PREFIX	Modifiers appear before time tokens	the, about	48
SUFFIX	Modifiers appear after time tokens	ago, old	2
LINKAGE	Link two time tokens	and, or, to, –	4
IN_ARTICLE	Indefinite articles	a, an	2
COMMA	Comma	,	1
Numeral			
NUMERAL	Numbers, ordinals	20, third	–

and are summarized in Table 4.1. Token types to tokens is like POS tags to words. For example, "February" has a POS tag of NNP and a token type of MONTH.

Time Token We define 15 token types for time tokens and use the names for token types similar to the Joda-Time classes:[1] DECADE (-), YEAR (-), SEASON (5), MONTH (12), WEEK (7), DATE (-), TIME (-), DAY_TIME (27), TIMELINE (12), HOLIDAY (20), PERIOD (9), DURATION (-), TIME_UNIT (15), TIME_ZONE (6), and ERA (2). The number in "(·)" represents the number of distinct tokens that are grouped under this token type. "–" indicates that this token type involves changing digits and cannot be counted.

---

[1] http://www.joda.org/joda-time/.

Modifier We define 3 token types for modifiers according to their possible positions relative to time tokens. Those modifiers that appear before time tokens are defined as PREFIX (48), while those modifiers that appear after time tokens are defined as SUFFIX (2). LINKAGE (4) links two time tokens. Besides, we define two special token types for modifiers, namely, COMMA (1) for the comma "," and IN_ARTICLE (2) for the two indefinite articles "a" and "an."

TimeML [6] and TimeBank [7] do not treat most prepositions (e.g., "on'' and "at") as part of time expressions. SynTime follows the standards of TimeML and TimeBank and therefore does not group those prepositions under our defined token types.

Numeral Numbers and ordinals in time expressions can be a time token, such as the "10" in "October 10, 2016," or a modifier, such as the "10" in "10 days." We define the token type NUMERAL (–) to group ordinals and numbers.

SynTime Initialization SynTime is initiated by importing token regular expressions from SUTime,[2] which is a state-of-the-art rule-based tagger that achieves the highest recall in TempEval-3 [2, 3]. Specifically, we collect from SUTime only its tokens and token regular expressions, and discard its other rules of recognizing full time expressions.

4.2 Time Expression Recognition

SynTime designs a small set of heuristic rules working on these defined token types to recognize time expressions. This recognition process mainly includes three steps: (1) time token identification, (2) time segment identification, and (3) time expression extraction.

4.2.1 Time Token Identification

Identifying time tokens is simple and straightforward, through matching the words in raw text with the token regular expressions grouped in SynTime. Some words might cause ambiguity. For example, the word "May" can be a modal verb, or a noun indicating the fifth month of a year. To filter out these ambiguous words, we employ the information of POS tags, which are obtained by using Stanford POS Tagger.[3] The strategy of using POS tags to identify the instances of defined token types is based on Characteristic 4 that is illustrated in Sect. 3.1.2.

---

[2]https://github.com/stanfordnlp/CoreNLP/tree/master/src/edu/stanford/nlp/time/rules.
[3]http://nlp.stanford.edu/software/tagger.shtml.

In this step, besides the time tokens are identified and assigned with their token types, the modifier and numeral words are also identified and assigned with their token types, if these words are matched with any of the modifier and numeral regular expressions. In the next two steps, SynTime will no longer work on specific tokens, but works on token types.

4.2.2   Time Segment Identification

The task of time segment identification is to search the surroundings of each identified time token for modifiers and numerals, and then gather the time token with its modifiers and numerals to form a time segment. The searching for modifiers and numerals is conducted under some simple heuristic rules in which the key idea is to expand the boundaries of time tokens.

At first, each time token is treated as a time segment. If it is either a **PERIOD** or a **DURATION**, then there is no need to further search. Otherwise, search its left-hand side and its right-hand side for modifiers and numerals. For the left-hand side searching, if encounter a **PREFIX** or a **NUMERAL** or an **IN_ARTICLE**, then continue searching. For the right-hand side searching, if encounter a **SUFFIX** or a **NUMERAL**, then continue searching. Both the left- and right-hand side searchings stop when encountering a **COMMA** or a **LINKAGE** or a non-modifier or non-numeral word (i.e., a word that is neither identified as a time token nor a modifier nor a numeral). The left-hand side searching for a time token does not exceed its previous time token; the right-hand side searching does not exceed its subsequent time token. A time segment consists of exactly one time token and zero or some modifiers or numerals.

A special kind of time segments does not contain any time token; instead, they depend on other time segments appearing nearby them. For example, the sequence "8–20 days" is assigned with the token types "**NUMERAL LINKAGE NUMERAL TIME_UNIT**," in which "**LINKAGE**/to **NUMERAL**/20 **TIME_UNIT**/days" is identified as a time segment while "**NUMERAL**/8 **LINKAGE**/to" is identified as a dependent time segment without any time token (see Fig. 4.2e).

4.2.3   Time Expression Extraction

The task of time expression extraction is to extract time expressions from the identified time segments, in which the key step is to determine whether to merge two adjacent or overlapping time segments into a new time segment.

We scan the time segments in a sentence from the beginning to the end. A stand-alone time segment is extracted as a time expression (see Fig. 4.2a). The focus is to deal with two or more time segments that are adjacent or overlapping. If two time segments s_1 and s_2 are adjacent, then merge them to form a new time segment s_1 (see

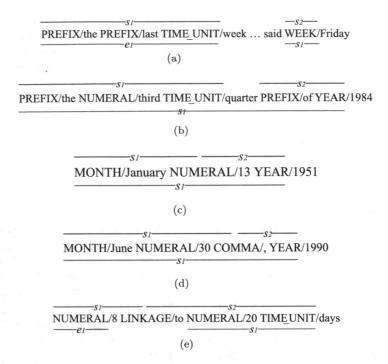

Fig. 4.2 Examples of time segments and time expressions. The labels s_1 and s_2 indicate time segments, while the label e_1 indicates time expressions. (**a**) A stand-alone time segment is extracted as a time expression. (**b**) Merge two adjacent time segments into a new time segment. (**c**) Merge overlapping time segments into a new time segment. (**d**) Merge two overlapping time segments into a new time segment. (**e**) A time segment and a dependent time segment

Fig. 4.2b). Consider the case that s_1 and s_2 overlap at a shared boundary. According to our strategy of time segment identification, the shared boundary can be a modifier or a numeral. If the shared boundary is neither a COMMA nor a LINKAGE, then merge s_1 and s_2 (see Fig. 4.2c). If the shared boundary is a LINKAGE, then extract s_1 as a time expression and continue scanning. When the shared boundary is a COMMA, merge s_1 and s_2 only if the COMMA's previous token and next token simultaneously satisfy the following three conditions: (1) the previous token is a time token or a NUMERAL, (2) the next token is a time token, and (3) the token types of the previous token and the next token are not the same (see Fig. 4.2d).

Although Fig. 4.2 shows these examples as the identified token types together with their specific tokens, we should note that heuristic rules only work on these token types and are independent of specific tokens. After the step of time expression extraction, a time expression is exported from a sequences of token types (which is at the type level) as a sequence of specific tokens (which is at the token level) (see Fig. 4.3f–h). Figure 4.3 shows eight key steps to demonstrate how SynTime recognizes the sequence "the third quart of 1984" as a time expressions in practice.

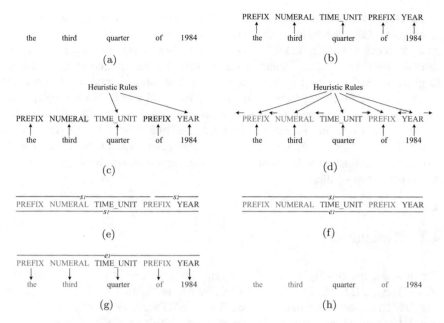

Fig. 4.3 Key steps of how SynTime recognizes a sequence as a time expression. (**a**) At the beginning, it is a sequence of specific tokens. (**b**) Firstly, assign these tokens with token types by simply looking up them at the token regular expressions. (**c**) Then, identify time tokens through the records of their token types when assigning token types to tokens. (**d**) After that, search the surroundings of time tokens for modifiers and numerals to form time segments. (**e**) Merge two adjacent time segments into a new time segment. (**f**) Extract a stand-alone time segment a time expression. This time expression is now at the type level. (**g**) Export a sequence of specific tokens from the sequence of token types as a time expression. (**h**) Finally, we get the recognized time expression at the token level

4.3   SynTime Expansion

SynTime can be expanded by simply adding new keywords or new token regular expressions under our defined token types without changing any rule. The expansion requires these added keywords and token regular expressions to be annotated manually. We apply the initial SynTime on the manually annotated time expressions from the training text and list those words that are not covered. Whether an uncovered word will be added to SynTime is manually determined. The rule for determination is that the added words can not cause ambiguity and should be generic. The WikiWars dataset contains a few examples like this: "The time Arnold reached Quebec City." Words in this example are extremely descriptive, and we do not collect them. On the other hand, tweets contain many informal variants and abbreviations in time expressions; for example, "2day" and "tday" are two popular spellings of "today." Such kind of informal variants and abbreviations are collected.

According to our analysis described in Characteristic 3, not many words are used to express time information, therefore, the manual addition of keywords will not cost too much effort. In addition, we find that even in tweets people tend to use formal words. In a set of Twitter word clusters that are trained from 56 million English tweets,[4] the most frequent used words are those formal words, and their frequencies are much higher than the ones of informal words. For example, in the cluster of "today,"[5] the most frequent word is the formal one "today," which occurs 1,220,829 times, while the second most frequent one "2day" occurs only 34,827 times. The low rate of informal words (e.g., about only 4% informal words in the "today" cluster) suggests that even in an informal environment, the manual addition of keywords costs little.

4.4 Evaluation

We evaluate the quality of SynTime against four state-of-the-art baselines (i.e., HeidelTime, SUTime, ClearTK-TimeML (short as "ClearTK" for convenience), and UWTime) on three datasets (i.e., TE-3, WikiWars, and Tweets). WikiWars is a domain-specific dataset about famous wars. TE-3 and WikiWars are the two datasets in formal text while the Tweets dataset is in informal text. In experiments, we implement SynTime in two versions: SynTime-I and SynTime-E. SynTime-I is the initial version, while SynTime-E is an expanded version of SynTime-I by adding keywords under our defined token types from the training text.

4.4.1 Setup

Datasets We use the following three datasets in our experiments: TE-3, WikiWars, and Tweets. The TE-3 dataset uses the TimeBank corpus as its training set and the TE3-Platinum corpus as its test set. TimeBank consists of 183 news articles and TE3-Platinum consists of 20 new articles; they are comprehensive corpora in formal text and are described in the TempEval-3 competition [11]. Although these two corpora are used in the same competition, they are collected independently. WikiWars is a domain-specific dataset in formal text, consisting of 22 English Wikipedia articles about famous wars [5]. Tweets is our manually labeled dataset that are collected from Twitter [13]. The three datasets are detailed in Sect. 3.1.1.

Compared Methods We compare SynTime with the following state-of-the-art methods: HeidelTime [8], SUTime [2], ClearTK [1] and UWTime [4]. HeidelTime

---

[4]http://www.cs.cmu.edu/~ark/TweetNLP/cluster_viewer.html.
[5]http://www.cs.cmu.edu/~ark/TweetNLP/paths/01111110010.html.

and SUTime are rule-based methods and use predefined deterministic rules and achieve the best results in the relaxed match, while ClearTK [1] uses a CRFs framework with the BIO scheme and achieves the best result in the strict match in the TempEval-3 competition [11]. UWTime uses combinatory categorial grammar (CCG) to predefine linguistic structure for time expressions and achieves better results than HeidelTime on the TE-3 and WikiWars datasets [4]. When testing HeidelTime on the Tweets dataset, we use its Colloquial setting which is designed for informal text. When training ClearTK and UWTime on the Tweets dataset, we try the following two settings: (1) training it on only the training set of Tweets, (2) training it on the TimeBank dataset and the Tweets training set together. The second setting achieves slightly better results and we report the results of this setting.

Evaluation Metrics We follow the TempEval-3 competition and use its evaluation toolkit[6] to report results in terms of *Strict Match* and *Relaxed Match* [11] under the three standard metrics: *Precision* (*Pr.*), *Recall* (*Re.*), and F_1. Strict match means exact match between the recognized time expressions and the ground-truth time expressions while relaxed match means that there exist certain overlap between the recognized ones and the ground-truth ones. *Pr.*, *Re.* and f_1 are defined by Eqs. (4.1), (4.2), and (4.3), respectively.

$$Pr. = \frac{TP}{TP + FP} \qquad (4.1)$$

$$Re. = \frac{TP}{TP + FN} \qquad (4.2)$$

$$F_1 = \frac{2 \times Pr. \times Re.}{Pr. + Re.} \qquad (4.3)$$

where TP (true-positive) denotes the number of time expressions that are recognized by the model and simultaneously appear the ground-truth, FP (false-positive) denotes the number of time expressions that are recognized by the model but do not appear in the ground-truth, while FN (false-negative) denotes the number of time expressions appearing in the ground-truth but are not recognized by the model.

4.4.2 Experimental Results

Table 4.2 presents the overall performance of SynTime and the four baselines on the three datasets. Among the total 18 measures, SynTime-I and SynTime-E achieve 11 best results and 12 s best results. Except the strict match on the WikiWars

---

[6]http://www.cs.rochester.edu/~naushad/tempeval3/tools.zip.

Table 4.2 Overall performance of SynTime and the four baselines on the three datasets. Within each metric, the best result is highlighted in boldface while the second best is underlined. Some results are reported directly from their original papers indicated by the references

Dataset	Method	Strict match			Relaxed match		
		Pr.	*Re.*	F_1	*Pr.*	*Re.*	F_1
TimeBank	HeidelTime [9]	83.85	78.99	81.34	93.08	87.68	90.30
	SUTime [3]	78.72	80.43	79.57	89.36	91.30	90.32
	ClearTK[1]	85.90	79.70	82.70	93.75	86.96	90.23
	UWTime [4]	86.10	80.40	83.10	**94.60**	88.40	91.40
	SynTime-I	<u>91.43</u>	<u>92.75</u>	<u>92.09</u>	<u>94.29</u>	**95.65**	**94.96**
	SynTime-E	**91.49**	**93.48**	**92.47**	93.62	**95.65**	<u>94.62</u>
WikiWars	HeidelTime[10]	**88.20**	78.50	<u>83.10</u>	95.80	85.40	90.30
	SUTime	78.61	76.69	76.64	95.74	89.57	92.55
	ClearTK	87.69	<u>80.28</u>	**83.82**	<u>96.80</u>	90.54	**93.56**
	UWTime [4]	**87.70**	78.80	83.00	**97.60**	87.60	92.30
	SynTime-I	80.00	80.22	80.11	92.16	<u>92.41</u>	92.29
	SynTime-E	79.18	**83.47**	81.27	90.49	**95.39**	<u>92.88</u>
Tweets	HeidelTime	**89.58**	72.88	80.37	95.83	77.97	85.98
	SUTime	76.03	77.97	76.99	88.43	90.68	89.54
	ClearTK	86.83	75.11	80.54	<u>96.59</u>	83.54	89.59
	UWTime	88.54	72.03	79.44	**96.88**	78.81	86.92
	SynTime-I	<u>89.52</u>	<u>94.07</u>	<u>91.74</u>	93.55	<u>98.31</u>	<u>95.87</u>
	SynTime-E	89.20	**94.49**	**91.77**	93.20	**98.78**	**95.88**

dataset, both SynTime-I and SynTime-E achieve the F_1 above 91%. For the relaxed match on all the three datasets, SynTime-I and SynTime-E achieve the recalls above 92%. The high recalls are consistent with Characteristic 2 that more than 91.81% of time expressions contain at least one time token (see Table 3.2). This indicates that SynTime covers most of time tokens. On the Tweets dataset, SynTime-I and SynTime-E achieve exceptionally good performance; their F_1 reaches 91.74% with an absolute 11.37% improvement in the strict match and 95.87% with an absolute 6.33% improvement in the relaxed match. The reasons are that in the informal environment people tend to use time expressions in their minimum length (62.91% one-word time expressions in Tweets; see Fig. 3.1), the size of time-related keywords is small (only 64 distinct time tokens; see Table 3.4), and even in tweets people tend to use formal words (see Sect. 4.3 for our finding about informal variants and abbreviations from a set of Twitter word clusters). For the precision, SynTime-I and SynTime-E achieve comparable results with the baselines in the strict match and performs slightly poorer in the relaxed match.

Next we discuss the comparison between the initial version SynTime-I and the four compared methods as well as the comparison between the expanded version SynTime-E and SynTime-I.

SynTime-I vs. Compared Methods On the TimeBank dataset, SynTime-I achieves the F_1 of 92.09% in the strict match and the one of 94.96% in the relaxed match. On the Tweets dataset, SynTime-I achieves the F_1 of 91.74% and 95.87%, respectively. It outperforms all the baseline methods. The reason is that for the two rule-based time taggers, their rules are designed in a fixed way that lacks flexibility. For example, SUTime can recognize the time expression "1 year" but not the one "year 1." For the two learning-based baseline, some of their features actually hurt the modeling. Time expressions involve quite many changing digits which by themselves affect the pattern recognition and modeling learning. For example, it is difficult to build a connection between the two time expressions "May 22, 1986" and "February 01, 1989" at the word level or the character level. One suggestion is to consider a type-based learning method that can use the type information. For example, the above two time expressions refer to the same pattern of "MONTH NUMERAL COMMA YEAR" at the level of token types. Part-of-speech (POS) is a kind of type information; the above two time expressions refer to the same pattern of "NNP CD, CD." According to our analysis, however, POS tags cannot distinguish time expressions from common words (see Characteristic 4). Features need carefully designing. On the WikiWars dataset, SynTime-I achieves competitive results in both matches. The reason is that time expressions in the WikiWars dataset include many prepositions and quite a few descriptive time expressions. SynTime cannot fully recognize these kinds of time expressions because it follows the standards of TimeML and TimeBank.

SynTime-E vs. SynTime-I Table 4.3 lists the number of time tokens and modifiers that are added to the SynTime-I so as to get the SynTime-E. On the TimeBank and Tweets datasets, only a few tokens are added, the corresponding results are affected slightly. This confirms that the number of time tokens is small, and that SynTime-I covers most time tokens. On the WikiWars dataset, because much more tokens are added, SynTime-E performs much better than SynTime-I, especially in the recall. SynTime-E improves the recall by absolute 3.25% in the strict match and by absolute 2.98% in the relaxed match. This indicates that with more words added from specific domains (e.g., the WikiWars dataset about war), SynTime can significantly improve the performance.

Table 4.3 Number of time tokens and modifiers added for expansion

Dataset	No. of time tokens	No. of modifiers
TimeBank	3	5
WikiWars	16	21
Tweets	3	2

4.5 Limitations

There are two possible limitations in SynTime. Firstly, SynTime assumes that all the time expressions appearing in text are correct. In daily life, however, people might write an invalid time expression (e.g., "31 February 2008") and SynTime cannot exclude such invalid time expressions but instead recognizes them as valid ones. Secondly, SynTime assumes that words are tokenized and POS tagged correctly. In reality, however, the tokenized and tagged words are not that perfect, due to the limitation of the used tool. For example, Stanford POS Tagger assigns VBD to the word "sat" in the sequence "friday or sat" while the word should be tagged as NNP. These incorrect tokenized tokens and POS tags affect the final performance.

References

1. Bethard S (2013) Cleartk-timeml: a minimalist approach to tempeval 2013. In: Proceedings of the 7th international workshop on semantic evaluation, p 10–14
2. Chang AX, Manning CD (2012) Sutime: a library for recognizing and normalizing time expressions. In: Proceedings of 8th international conference on language resources and evaluation, p 3735–3740
3. Chang AX, Manning CD (2013) Sutime: evaluation in TempEval-3. In: Proceedings of the second joint conference on lexical and computational semantics (SEM), p 78–82
4. Lee K, Artzi Y, Dodge J, Zettlemoyer L (2014) Context-dependent semantic parsing for time expressions. In: Proceedings of the 52th annual meeting of the association for computational linguistics, p 1437–1447
5. Mazur P, Dale R (2010) Wikiwars: a new corpus for research on temporal expressions. In: Proceedings of the 2010 conference on empirical methods in natural language processing, p 913–922
6. Pustejovsky J, Castano J, Ingria R, Sauri R, Gaizauskas R, Setzer A, Katz G, Radev D (2003) Timeml: robust specification of event and temporal expressions in text. New Dir Quest Answering 3:28–34
7. Pustejovsky J, Hanks P, Sauri R, See A, Gaizauskas R, Setzer A, Sundheim B, Radev D, Day D, Ferro L, Lazo M (2003) The timebank corpus. Corpus Linguist 2003:647–656
8. Strötgen J, Gertz M (2010) Heideltime: high quality rule-based extraction and normalization of temporal expressions. In: Proceedings of the 5th international workshop on semantic evaluation (SemEval'10). Association for Computational Linguistics, Stroudsburg, p 321–324
9. Strötgen J, Zell J, Gertz M (2013) Heideltime: tuning English and developing Spanish resources. In: Proceedings of the second joint conference on lexical and computational semantics (SEM), p 15–19
10. Strötgen J, Bogel T, Zell J, Armiti A, Canh TV, Gertz M (2014) Extending heideltime for temporal expressions referring to historic dates. In: Proceedings of the 9th international conference on language resources and evaluation, p 2390–2397
11. UzZaman N, Llorens H, Derczynski L, Verhagen M, Allen J, Pustejovsky J (2013) Semeval-2013 task 1: TempEval-3: evaluating time expressions, events, and temporal relations. In: Proceedings of the 7th international workshop on semantic evaluation, p 1–9
12. Zhong X (2020) Time expression and named entity analysis and recognition. PhD thesis, Nanyang Technological University, Singapore
13. Zhong X, Sun A, Cambria E (2017) Time expression analysis and recognition using syntactic token types and general heuristic rules. In: Proceedings of the 55th annual meeting of the association for computational linguistics, Vancouver, vol 1, p 420–429

Chapter 5
TOMN: Constituent-Based Tagging Scheme

Abstract The characteristics of time expressions drive us to design a learning-based method named TOMN to model time expressions. TOMN defines a constituent-based tagging scheme named TOMN scheme with four tags, namely T, O, M, and N, indicating the constituents of time expression, namely Time token, Modifier, Numeral, and the words Outside time expression. In modeling, TOMN assigns a word with a TOMN tag under conditional random fields with minimal features. Essentially, our constituent-based TOMN scheme overcomes the problem of *inconsistent tag assignment* that is caused by the conventional position-based tagging schemes (e.g., BIO scheme and BILOU scheme). Evaluation shows that TOMN is equally or more effective than state-of-the-art methods on various datasets, and much more robust on cross-datasets.

Keywords Constituent-based tagging scheme · Position-based tagging scheme · Inconsistent tag assignment

TOMN defines a constituent-based tagging scheme to model time expressions under a framework of conditional random fields (CRFs). Figure 5.1 displays the overview of TOMN that mainly includes three parts: TOMN scheme, TmnRegex, and time expression recognition. The TOMN scheme consists of four tags. TmnRegex is a set of regular expressions about time-related tokens. Time expressions are modeled under a CRFs framework with the help of TmnRegex and the TOMN scheme as well as minimal features derived from context according to their characteristics described in Sect. 3.1.2 [23, 24].

Fig. 5.1 Overview of
TOMN. Top-left side shows
the TOMN scheme,
consisting of four tags.
Bottom-left side is the
TmnRegex, a set of regular
expressions for time-related
words. Right-hand side shows
the time expression modeling,
with TmnRegex and TOMN
scheme

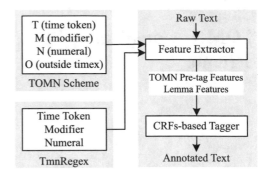

5.1   TOMN Scheme

Characteristic 5 states that time expressions are formed by loose structure and
suggests us to explore an appropriate tagging scheme to model time expressions.
We therefore define a constituent-based tagging scheme termed TOMN scheme with
four tags: T, O, M, and N; they indicate the constituent words of time expressions,
namely *time tokens*, modifiers, *numerals*, and the words appearing *outside* time
expressions.

Conventional tagging schemes like the BIO scheme[1] [16] and the BILOU
scheme[2] [14] are based on *the positions within labeled chunks*. BIO indicates the
beginning, inside, and outside words of a chunk; BILOU indicates a unit-word
chunk, and the beginning, inside, last words of a multi-word chunk. By contrast,
our TOMN scheme is based on *the constituents of labeled chunks*, indicating the
constituent words of time expressions. Next, we use the BILOU scheme as the
representative of these conventional position-based tagging schemes for analysis.

Using the BILOU scheme for time expression modeling leads to the problem
of inconsistent tag assignment.[3] Characteristic 5 demonstrates that time expressions
are formed by loose structure which exhibits in the two aspects of loose collocations
and exchangeable order. Under the BILOU scheme, both loose collocations and
exchangeable order lead to inconsistent tag assignment. Suppose "September,"
"September 2006," "2006 September," and "1 September 2006" are four manually
labeled time expressions in training data. During feature extraction, they are
assigned with the BILOU tags as "September/U," "September/B 2006/L," "2006/B
September/L," and "1/B September/I 2006/L" (see Fig. 1.2a). These four "September" have the same word (i.e., the word itself) and express the same meaning (i.e.,

---

[1]The BIO scheme denotes the standard IOB2 scheme described in [16].

[2]The BILOU scheme is also widely known as the IOBES scheme and the BIOES scheme.

[3]A typical supervised-learning procedure involves tag assignment in two stages: feature extraction
during the training stage and sequence tagging during the test stage. We focus on the training stage
to analyze the impact of tag assignment in different types of tagging schemes.

the ninth month of a year), but because they appear in different positions within labeled time expressions, they are assigned with different tags (i.e., U, B, L, and I).

The inconsistent tag assignment causes difficulty for statistical models to model time expressions. Firstly, inconsistent tag assignment reduces the predictive power of lexicon. A word that is assigned with different tags causes confusion for statistical models to model the word. If a word is assigned with different tags in an equal number, then the word itself cannot provide any useful information to determine which tag should be assigned to it. Reducing the predictive power of lexicon indicates reducing the predictive power of time tokens, and this contradicts Characteristic 2 which states that time tokens can distinguish time expressions from common text. Secondly, inconsistent tag assignment may cause another problem: tag imbalance. If a tag of a word dominates in training data, then all the instances of that word in test data will be predicted as that tag. For example, "1 September 2006" can be written as "September 1, 2006" in some cultures. If the training data are collected from the text with the style of "1 September 2006" in which most "September" are assigned with I, then it is difficult for a trained model to correctly predict the data collected from text with the style of "September 1, 2006" in which "September" should be predicted as B.

Our TOMN scheme instead overcomes the problem of inconsistent tag assignment. The TOMN scheme assigns a tag to a word according to the constituent role that the word plays in time expressions. Since our TmnRegex well defines the constituent words of time expressions (see Sect. 5.2) and the same word plays the same constituent role in time expressions, therefore, the same word is assigned with the same TOMN tag, regardless of its frequency and its positions within time expressions. For example, our TOMN scheme assigns the above four time expressions as "September/T," "2006/T September/T," "September/T 2006/T," and "1/N September/T 2006/T" (see Fig. 1.2b). We can see that these four "September" are consistently assigned with the same tag of "T" and statistical models need only to model them as "T," without any confusion. With consistent tag assignment, our TOMN scheme protects the predictive power of time tokens and avoids the potential tag imbalance.

In addition, our TOMN scheme models a word by fewer tags than the BILOU scheme. The BILOU scheme typically models a time token by four tags (i.e., U, B, L, or I) and models a modifier or numeral by five tags (i.e., U, B, L, I, or O), while our TOMN scheme models a time token by only one tag (i.e., T) and models a modifier or numeral by two tags (i.e., M or N if the modifier or numeral appears inside time expressions and O if it appears outside time expressions). Compared with the BILOU scheme, our TOMN scheme reduces the computational complexity for training a model.

5.2   TmnRegex

Characteristic 3 indicates that only a small group of words that are used in time expressions. TOMN employs three time-related token types, namely time token, modifier, and numeral, to group those words. The three token types are the same as the ones defined in SynTime [25] and correspond to three of the above four tags (i.e., T, M, and N) defined in the TOMN scheme.

Time tokens explicitly express information about time, such as year (e.g., "2006"), month (e.g., "September"), date (e.g., "2006-09-01"), and time units (e.g., "month"). Modifiers are the words that modify time tokens and appear around them. For example, the two modifiers "the" and "last" modify the time token "month" in the time expression "the last month." Numerals include ordinals and numbers, except those that are recognized as year (e.g., "2006"). Token types are defined on top of specific tokens themselves and are not necessarily relevant to their context. For example, "2006" alone expresses time information, so it is treated as a time token; on the other hand, although the "1" in the time expression "1 September 2006" implies the day, itself alone does not express time information, so it is treated as a numeral.

These three token types with those words they group constitute a set of token regular expressions, which is denoted by TmnRegex. TmnRegex is constructed by importing token regular expressions for its time token, modifier, and numeral from the state-of-the-art rule-based time tagger SUTime.[4] Like SynTime, TmnRegex collects from SUTime only the regular expressions at the level of tokens and discards its regular expressions for the whole time expressions. In summary, TmnRegex contains only 115 distinct time tokens, 57 distinct modifiers, and 58 numerals, without counting those words with changing digits.

5.3   Time Expression Recognition

Time expression recognition mainly consists of two stages: (1) feature extraction and (2) model learning and sequence tagging. When extracting features we set a guideline that the extracted features should be able to help distinguish time expressions from common text and help build connections among time expressions.

5.3.1   Feature Extraction

The features we extract for time expression modeling include two kinds: TOMN pre-tag features and lemma features. During the feature extraction, we use w_i to denote the i-th word in the text.

---

[4]https://github.com/stanfordnlp/CoreNLP/tree/master/src/edu/stanford/nlp/time/rules.

TOMN Pre-tag Features Characteristic 2 states that time tokens can distinguish time expressions from common text while modifiers and numerals cannot, therefore, how to leverage the information of these words becomes crucial. In our consideration, they are treated as pre-tag features under our TOMN scheme. Specifically, a time token is pre-tagged by the tag of T, a modifier is pre-tagged by M, and a numeral is pre-tagged by N; other common words are pre-tagged by O. The assignment of pre-tags for words is conducted by simply looking up them at the token regular expressions grouped in TmnRegex.

The last four columns of Table 3.3 indicate that modifiers and numerals constantly appear in time expressions and in common text. To distinguish where a modifier or numeral appears, we conduct a checking for the those words that are pre-tagged as modifiers and numerals (i.e., those words with pre-tags of M or N; they are simply denoted by M/N in the remaining of this paragraph) to record whether or not they directly or indirectly modify any time token. "Indirectly" here means a M/N together with other M/N modifies a time token; for example, in the time expression "last two months," the modifier "last" (M) together with the modifier "two" (N) modifies the time token "months" (T). This checking is a loop searching relying on the identified time tokens. For each identified time token (i.e., those words with a pre-tag of T), we search its left-hand side without exceeding the previous time token and search its right-hand side without exceeding the next time token. When searching a side of a time token, if encounter a M/N, then record this M/N and continue searching; if encounter a word that is not a M/N, then stop the searching for this side of this time token. After the checking, those M/N that modify time tokens are recorded while those M/N that do not modify any time token will not recorded. For example, the modifier "two" (M) in the time expression "two months" is recorded because it modifies the time token "months" (T); by contrast, in the sequence "two apples," the modifier "two" (N) will not recorded because it does not modify any time token but only modifies the common word "apples." The checking result is treated as a feature for modeling.

For the TOMN pre-tag features, we extract them in a 5-word window of the current word w_i for w_i, namely the pre-tags of w_{i-2}, w_{i-1}, w_i, w_{i+1}, and w_{i+2}. For the checking feature, we only consider whether the current word w_i is recorded or not.

In the training phase, we consider the TOMN pre-tag features for only those words appearing in labeled time expressions. In the test phase, we extract the TOMN pre-tag features for all the words in the whole text.

Lemma Features The lemma features include the word shape in a 5-word window of w_i, namely the lemmas of w_{i-2}, w_{i-1}, w_i, w_{i+1}, and w_{i+2}. If w_i contains changing digit(s), then its lemma is set by its token type. For example, the lemma of "20:16" is set by TIME. We use the following five special token types as lemma for those words with changing digits: YEAR, DATE, TIME, DECADE, and NUMERAL. The lemma features can help build connections among time expressions; for example, the two different words "20:16" and "19:25:33" are connected by the same lemma TIME at the type level.

Table 5.1 Extracted features for word w_i in named entity modeling

1.	TOMN pre-tag features in a 5-word window of w_i, namely the pre-tags of w_{i-2}, w_{i-1}, w_i, w_{i+1}, and w_{i+2}
2.	If w_i is a M or N, then check whether or not it directly or indirectly modifies any time token
3.	Lemma features in a 5-word window of w_i

The lemma features are extracted for all the words in the whole text in both the training phase and the test phase.

We do not consider the features of characters and word variants because they cannot help build connections among time expressions but hurt the modeling learning and pattern recognition. For example, "Sept." is an abbreviation of "September" and both of them express the same meaning but computer does not treat them as the same thing.

We also do not consider the POS features and other syntactic features. Characteristic 4 indicates that POS tags cannot distinguish time expressions from common text, and our experiments confirm that adding POS tags as features does not improve the performance. On the other hand, Characteristic 5 shows that time expressions are formed by loose structure, which together with Characteristic 4 suggests that other syntactic features (e.g., syntactic dependency) that rely on POS tags and fixed linguistic structure cannot provide extra useful information for a CRFs-based learning method, which already considers the dependency, to distinguish time expressions from common text. We therefore do not use those syntactic features in our model.

Table 5.1 summarizes the features that are extracted for word w_i for time expression modeling. Typically up to 11 features are extracted for a word.

Feature Values For the TOMN pre-tag features, we extract them as separate features with binary values. The theory of scales of measurement suggests that non-ordinal attributes should be transformed onto separate dimensions [17].The TOMN pre-tag features and the checking features are non-ordinal, therefore, they are extracted as separate features. For the lemma features, we follow their traditional use to incorporate multiple values under a feature.

5.3.2 Model Learning and Tagging

TOMN models time expressions under a CRFs framework [8] with the extracted features described above. In implementation, we use Stanford Tagger[5] to obtain the lemma features and use CRFSuite[6] with the default setting for model learning

---

[5]http://nlp.stanford.edu/software/tagger.shtml.

[6]http://www.chokkan.org/software/crfsuite/.

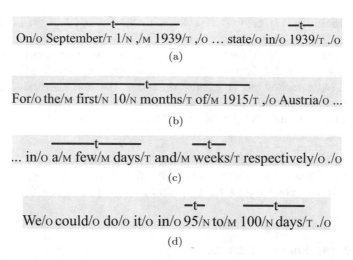

(a)

(b)

(c)

(d)

Fig. 5.2 Examples of time expression extraction. The label *t* indicates time expressions. (**a**) T, M, and N words together form a time expression. (**b**) T, M, and N words together form a time expression. (**c**) Linker "and" separates two time expressions. (**d**) Linker "to" separates two time expressions

and sequence tagging. During sequence tagging, one word is assigned with one of TOMN tags, namely T, O, M, or N. Note that the TOMN scheme is used in feature extraction as a kind of pre-tag features as well as in sequence tagging as the labeling tags.

Time Expression Extraction After sequence tagging, those T, M, and N words (i.e., non-O words) that appear together are extracted as a time expression. See Fig. 5.2a, b. A special kind of modifiers (i.e., the linkers "to," "–," "or," and "and") separates those non-O words into two or more parallel time expressions. See Fig. 5.2c, d.

5.4   Evaluation

We conduct experiments to evaluate the quality of TOMN on three datasets (i.e., TE-3, WikiWars, and Tweets) in comparison with five state-of-the-art methods (i.e., HeidelTime, SUTime, SynTime, ClearTK and UWTime).

5.4.1   Setup

Datasets We use the same three datasets in our experiments as the ones used in SynTime. These three datasets are detailed in Sects. 3.1.1 and 4.4.1.

Baseline Methods We compare TOMN with the five state-of-the-art methods: HeidelTime [18], SUTime [2], ClearTK [1], UWTime [10], and SynTime [25]. The first four methods are described in Sect. 4.4.1 while SynTime is our first method proposed for time expression recognition. In implementation, SynTime has two versions, a basic version and an expanded version. Because the expanded version requires extra manual annotation for each dataset, for fair comparison, we use the basic version to ensure that the token regular expressions used in SynTime and TOMN are comparable.

Evaluation Metrics We report results under *Strict Match* and *Relaxed Match* in the three standard metrics: *Precision* (*Pr.*), *Recall* (*Re.*), and F_1. They are the same as the metrics described in Sect. 4.4.1 and defined by Eqs. (4.1), (4.2), and (4.3).

5.4.2 Experimental Results

Table 5.2 reports the overall performance of TOMN and the five compared methods on the three experimental datasets. Among the total 18 measures, TOMN achieves 13 best or second best results. It performs better than SynTime which achieves 10

Table 5.2 Overall performance of TOMN and the five baselines on the three experimental datasets. Within each metric, the best result is highlighted in boldface while the second best is underlined. Some results are reported directly from their publicly available sources

Dataset	Method	Strict match			Relaxed Match		
		Pr.	*Re.*	F_1	*Pr.*	*Re.*	F_1
TE-3	HeidelTime[19]	83.85	78.99	81.34	93.08	87.68	90.30
	SUTime[3]	78.72	80.43	79.57	89.36	91.30	90.32
	SynTime[25]	91.43	**92.75**	**92.09**	94.29	**95.65**	**94.96**
	ClearTK[1]	85.90	79.70	82.70	93.75	86.96	90.23
	UWTime[10]	86.10	80.40	83.10	94.60	88.40	91.40
	TOMN	**92.59**	90.58	91.58	**95.56**	93.48	94.51
WikiWars	HeidelTime[20]	**88.20**	78.50	83.10	95.80	85.40	90.30
	SUTime	78.61	76.69	76.64	95.74	89.57	92.55
	SynTime[25]	80.00	80.22	80.11	92.16	**92.41**	92.29
	ClearTK	87.69	80.28	**83.82**	96.80	90.54	93.56
	UWTime[10]	87.70	78.80	83.00	**97.60**	87.60	92.30
	TOMN	84.57	**80.48**	82.47	96.23	92.35	**94.25**
Tweets	HeidelTime	**91.67**	74.26	82.05	96.88	78.48	86.71
	SUTime	77.69	79.32	78.50	88.84	90.72	89.77
	SynTime[25]	89.52	94.07	91.74	93.55	**98.31**	**95.87**
	ClearTK	86.83	75.11	80.54	96.59	83.54	89.59
	UWTime	88.36	70.76	78.59	**97.88**	78.39	87.06
	TOMN	90.69	**94.51**	**92.56**	93.52	97.47	95.45

best or second best results, and much better than other four baselines which achieve at most 4 best or second best results. For each measure, TOMN achieves either the best result or a comparable result with the best result. Especially for the F_1, TOMN performs the best in the strict F_1 on the Tweets dataset and in the relaxed F_1 on the WikiWars dataset. For other F_1, TOMN achieves the comparable results compared to the corresponding best results; most of the differences between their performance are less than 0.5%.

5.4.3 TOMN vs. Baseline Methods

We further compare TOMN with the rule-based baselines and the learning-based baselines.

TOMN vs. Rule-Based Baselines On the TE-3 and Tweets datasets, TOMN achieves comparable results with SynTime. On the WikiWars dataset, TOMN achieves the F_1 with absolute 2.0~2.3% increase in comparison with SynTime. This indicates that compared with SynTime, TOMN is equally effective on comprehensive data and more effective on domain-specific data. The reason is that the heuristic rules of SynTime are greedy for recalls at the cost of precisions, and such cost is expensive when it comes to domain-specific data. TOMN instead leverages statistical information from the whole corpus, which might miss some rare time expressions but helps recognize time expressions more precisely; especially in domain-specific data, the statistical information significantly improves the precisions at little cost of recalls. For HeidelTime and SUTime, except the strict F_1 on the WikiWars dataset, TOMN outperforms the two baselines on all the three datasets, with up to absolute 15.3% increase in recalls and up to absolute 12.0% increase in F_1. The reason is that these deterministic rules of HeidelTime and SUTime are designed in fixed manners that lack flexibility [25].

TOMN vs. Learning-Based Baselines Except the strict F_1 on the WikiWars dataset, TOMN outperforms ClearTK and UWTime on all the three datasets in all the recalls and all the F_1. Especially on the TE-3 and Tweets datasets, TOMN improves the recalls by at least absolute 9.8% in the strict match and at least absolute 5.1% in the relaxed match, and improves the F_1 by at least absolute 8.5% in the strict match and at least absolute 3.1% in the relaxed match. The reasons are that (1) the fixed linguistic structure that are predefined in UWTime cannot fully capture the loose structure of time expressions, (2) the BIO scheme used in ClearTK suffers from the problem of inconsistent tag assignment and reduces the predictive power of time tokens, and (3) some of their features (e.g., POS tags and syntactic dependency features) actually hurt the modeling learning and pattern recognition. For the strict F_1 on the WikiWars dataset, TOMN performs slightly poorer than these two learning-based methods, because TOMN uses the same token regular expressions as SynTime and follows TimeBank and SynTime to exclude most prepositions (except "of") from time expressions while some time expressions in the WikiWars dataset include those prepositions.

5.4.4 Cross-Dataset Performance

We conduct a series of cross-dataset experiments to evaluate the robustness of TOMN in comparison with the two learning-based methods that require training. In cross-dataset experiments, a method is trained on the training set of one dataset and then tested on the test sets of other datasets. Since these three datasets (i.e., TE-3, WikiWars, and Tweets) used in our experiments are quite diverse, the cross-dataset experiments can evaluate the robustness of a learning-based method. Table 5.3 presents the cross-dataset performance on the test set of the TE-3 dataset; Table 5.4 presents the performance on the test set of WikiWars; Table 5.5 on the test set of Tweets. For a convenient comparison, Table 5.3, 5.4, and 5.5 also present the performance on the single-dataset experiments. "Single-dataset" here means that the training set and the test set belong to the same dataset. The results of the single-dataset experiments are reported directly from Table 5.2, and they are indicated by the colored background in Table 5.3, 5.4, and 5.5.

Table 5.3 Cross-dataset performance on the test set of TE-3. "Training" indicates the dataset whose training set is used for training. Colored background indicates the single-dataset results

Training	Method	Strict match			Relaxed match		
		$Pr.$	$Re.$	F_1	$Pr.$	$Re.$	F_1
TE-3	ClearTK	85.90	79.70	82.70	93.75	86.96	90.23
	UWTime	86.10	80.40	83.10	94.60	88.40	91.40
	TOMN	**92.59**	**90.58**	**91.58**	**95.56**	**93.48**	**94.51**
WikiWars	ClearTK	65.67	63.77	64.71	87.31	84.78	86.03
	UWTime	76.92	72.46	74.63	88.46	83.33	85.82
	TOMN	**84.06**	**84.06**	**84.06**	**93.48**	**93.48**	**93.48**
Tweets	ClearTK	72.59	71.01	71.79	**93.33**	91.30	92.31
	UWTime	80.00	72.46	76.05	92.80	84.06	88.21
	TOMN	**85.42**	**89.13**	**87.23**	91.67	**95.65**	**93.62**

Table 5.4 Cross-dataset performance on the test set of WikiWars

Training	Method	Strict match			Relaxed match		
		$Pr.$	$Re.$	F_1	$Pr.$	$Re.$	F_1
TE-3	ClearTK	74.38	60.76	66.89	**97.54**	79.68	87.71
	UWTime	**87.01**	**79.34**	**83.00**	96.07	87.60	91.64
	TOMN	82.18	75.65	79.07	96.26	**87.93**	**91.90**
WikiWars	ClearTK	87.69	80.28	**83.82**	96.80	90.54	93.56
	UWTime	**87.70**	78.80	83.00	**97.60**	87.60	92.30
	TOMN	84.57	**80.48**	82.47	96.23	**92.35**	**94.25**
Tweets	ClearTK	57.75	54.73	56.20	91.93	87.12	**89.46**
	UWTime	**80.28**	62.81	**70.48**	**94.37**	73.83	82.84
	TOMN	60.29	**66.00**	63.02	84.74	**92.76**	88.57

Table 5.5 Cross-dataset performance on the test set of Tweets

Training	Method	Strict match			Relaxed match		
		Pr.	*Re.*	F_1	*Pr.*	*Re.*	F_1
TE-3	ClearTK	81.16	47.26	59.73	**97.10**	56.54	71.47
	UWTime	89.66	65.82	75.91	94.83	69.62	80.29
	TOMN	**92.92**	**88.61**	**90.71**	96.90	**92.41**	**94.60**
WikiWars	ClearTK	72.48	45.57	55.96	95.30	59.92	73.58
	UWTime	**87.43**	61.60	72.28	**95.81**	67.61	79.21
	TOMN	85.00	**86.08**	**85.53**	93.75	**94.94**	**94.34**
Tweets	ClearTK	86.83	75.11	80.54	96.59	83.54	89.59
	UWTime	88.36	70.76	78.59	**97.88**	78.39	87.06
	TOMN	**90.69**	**94.51**	**92.56**	93.52	**97.47**	**95.45**

On the test set of TE-3, TOMN achieves at least 84.0% in the strict F_1 and at least 93.4% in the relaxed F_1 (see the rows of WikiWars and Tweets in Table 5.3). On the test set of Tweets, TOMN achieves at least 85.5% in the strict F_1 and at least 94.3% in the relaxed F_1 (see the rows of TE-3 and WikiWars in Table 5.5). It significantly outperforms ClearTK and UWTime. On the test set of WikiWars, TOMN achieves comparable results with ClearTK and UWTime in the relaxed match but performs poorer than UWTime in the strict match. Especially when trained on the training set of Tweets, TOMN achieves only 63.0% in the strict F_1, which is absolute 7.5% lower than the one of UWTime (see the rows of TE-3 and Tweets in Table 5.4). Tweets contains many short time expressions (62.9% one-word time expressions; see Fig. 3.1) and uses fewer modifiers and numerals in time expressions, while WikiWars includes quite a few long time expressions (only 36.2% one-word time expressions) and some descriptive time expressions. For these reasons, when TOMN is trained on the training set of Tweets, it cannot fully recognize the long and descriptive time expressions in the test of WikiWars. UWTime instead predefines some linguistic structure, which contributes significantly to the exact recognition of those long and descriptive time expressions.

Let us look at the single-dataset and cross-dataset performance in the relaxed match. TOMN achieves similar performance, regardless of which dataset it is trained on. Specifically, in the relaxed F_1, TOMN achieves about 93.9% on the test of TE-3, about 91.6% on the test set of WikiWars, and about 94.8% on the one of Tweets. By contrast, ClearTK and UWTime perform relatively well on the single-dataset experiments but much worse on the cross-dataset experiments. Especially on the test of Tweets, their relaxed F_1 drops from at least 87.0% when they are trained on the training set of Tweets to at most 80.3% when they are trained on the training sets of other datasets. This demonstrates that TOMN is much more robust than ClearTK and UWTime.

The robustness of TOMN can be explained by Characteristics 2 and 3. Characteristic 2 indicates that time tokens are capable of predicting time expressions and Characteristic 3 indicates that time expressions highly overlap at their time tokens within an individual dataset and across different datasets. That means, the time tokens from one dataset can help recognize the time tokens from other datasets. Therefore, in terms of the relaxed match, the cross-dataset performance should be comparable to the single-dataset performance.

5.4.5   Factor Analysis

We conduct controlled experiments to analyze the impact of the TOMN scheme as labeling tags as well as the impact of the features that are used in TOMN. The experimental results are presented in Table 5.6.

Impact of the TOMN Labeling Tags To analyze the impact of the TOMN scheme as labeling tags, we keep all the features unchanged except change the labeling tags

Table 5.6 Performance of controlled experiments for the impact of factors. "BIO" denotes the systems that replace the TOMN labeling tags by the BIO tags while "BILOU" denotes the systems that replace by the BILOU tags. "*trad*" indicates the traditional strategy for time expression extraction while "*nono*" indicates the non-O strategy. "−" indicates that this kind of features that are removed from TOMN. "PreTag" denotes the TOMN pre-tag features while "Lemma" denotes the lemma features

Dataset	Method	Strict match			Relaxed match		
		$Pr.$	$Re.$	F_1	$Pr.$	$Re.$	F_1
TE-3	TOMN	**92.59**	**90.58**	**91.58**	95.56	93.48	**94.51**
	BIO$_{trad}$	83.06	74.64	78.63	94.35	84.78	89.31
	BIO$_{nono}$	84.68	76.09	80.15	94.35	84.78	89.31
	BILOU$_{trad}$	84.75	72.46	78.12	94.92	81.16	87.50
	BILOU$_{nono}$	86.44	73.91	79.69	94.92	81.16	87.50
	−PreTag	89.36	60.87	72.41	**95.74**	65.22	77.59
	−Lemma	81.56	83.33	82.44	92.20	**94.20**	93.19
WikiWars	TOMN	84.57	**80.48**	**82.47**	96.23	92.35	**94.25**
	BIO$_{trad}$	77.75	71.03	74.24	93.39	85.31	89.17
	BIO$_{nono}$	77.75	71.03	74.24	93.39	85.31	89.17
	BILOU$_{trad}$	79.56	72.03	75.61	93.56	84.71	88.91
	BILOU$_{nono}$	79.78	72.23	75.82	93.56	84.71	88.91
	−PreTag	**87.22**	70.02	77.68	**99.25**	79.68	88.39
	−Lemma	74.80	75.25	75.03	92.20	**92.56**	92.28
Tweets	TOMN	90.69	94.51	**92.56**	93.52	97.47	**95.45**
	BIO$_{trad}$	89.16	93.67	91.36	92.37	97.05	94.65
	BIO$_{nono}$	90.24	93.67	91.93	93.50	97.05	95.24
	BILOU$_{trad}$	89.37	**95.78**	92.46	92.13	**98.73**	95.32
	BILOU$_{nono}$	90.65	94.09	92.34	93.50	97.06	95.24
	−PreTag	**92.41**	61.60	73.92	**98.10**	65.40	78.48
	−Lemma	90.69	94.51	**92.56**	93.52	97.47	**95.45**

from the TOMN scheme to the BIO scheme to get a BIO system and change to the BILOU scheme to get a BILOU system. The BIO and BILOU systems use the same TOMN pre-tag features and lemma features that are used in TOMN.[7]

The tag assignment of the BIO and BILOU schemes during feature extraction in the training stage follows their traditional use. For example, a unit-word time expression is assigned with B under the BIO scheme while it is assigned with U under the BILOU scheme. When extracting time expressions from a tagged sequence in the test stage, we adopt two strategies. One strategy follows their traditional use in which time expressions are extracted according to the tags of words. For example, a U word under the BILOU scheme is extracted as a time expression. The other strategy follows the one used for TOMN in which those consecutive non-O words are extracted as a time expression (see Sect. 5.3.2). The traditional strategy is denoted by "*trad*" while the non-O strategy is denoted by "*nono*." The results of the BIO and BILOU systems are reported as respective "BIO" and "BILOU" in Table 5.6. We can see that the non-O strategy performs almost the same as the traditional strategy, and the BIO systems achieve comparable or slightly better results compared with the BILOU systems. The reason is as follows. Time expressions on average contain about two words (see Characteristic 1); in that case, the BILOU scheme is reduced approximately to the BLOU scheme and the BIO scheme is changed approximately to the BLO scheme. Between the BLOU scheme and the BLO scheme there is only slight difference; under the impact of inconsistent tag assignment and TOMN pre-tag features, this slight difference affects slightly to the performance. In what follows we do not distinguish the BILOU scheme from the BIO scheme and do not distinguish the non-O strategy from the traditional strategy; the four methods of BIO_{trad}, BIO_{nono}, $BILOU_{trad}$, and $BILOU_{nono}$ are simply represented by "BILOU."

On the TE-3 and WikiWars datasets, TOMN significantly outperforms BILOU. Specifically, TOMN achieves the recalls that are absolute 7.0~14.5% higher than those of BILOU, and achieves the F_1 that are absolute 5.0~11.4% higher than those of BILOU. The reason is that both loose collocations and exchangeable order of loose structure in time expressions lead the BILOU scheme to suffer from the problem of inconsistent tag assignment. Our constituent-based TOMN scheme instead overcomes that problem.

On the Tweets dataset, TOMN and BILOU achieve similar performance; the difference between their performance in most measures is less than 1%. The reason is that 62.9% of time expressions in the Tweets dataset are one-word time expressions (see Fig. 3.1) and 96.0% of time expressions contain time tokens (see Characteristic 1), and they together indicates that these one-word time expressions contain only time tokens. In that case, the TOMN scheme is reduced approximately

---

[7]The BIO and BILOU schemes can be extracted with other features, but our using the BIO and BILOU schemes here is to conduct controlled experiments to analyze the impact of the TOMN scheme as labeling tags, therefore, we extract the same features in TOMN for the BIO and BILOU schemes.

to the TO scheme and the BILOU scheme is reduced approximately to the UO scheme. Then the UO scheme becomes a constituent-based tagging scheme in which U models time tokens. It is equivalent to the TO scheme. (In that case, the BIO scheme is reduced approximately to the BO scheme in which B models time tokens. Then the BO scheme is equivalent to the TO scheme as well as the UO scheme.)

Impact of the TOMN Pre-tag Features To analyze the impact of the TOMN pre-tag features, we remove them from TOMN. After they are removed, although most of the precisions increase and even reach the highest scores, all the recalls and F_1 drop dramatically, with absolute 10.4~32.9% decreases in recalls and absolute 4.8~19.1% decreases in F_1. That means the TOMN pre-tag features significantly improve the performance and confirms the predictive power of time tokens. The results also validate that pre-tagging features is a good way to use the information of those lexicon. And our constituent-based TOMN scheme keeps the pre-tagging assignment consistent, just like the way that it keeps the labeling tag assignment consistent.

Impact of the Lemma Features When lemma features are removed from TOMN, the performance in the relaxed match on all the three datasets is affected slightly. The reason is that the TOMN pre-tag features provide useful information to recognize time tokens. The strict match on the TE-3 and WikiWars datasets decreases dramatically, which indicates that the lemma features heavily affect the recognition of modifiers and numerals. The strict match on the Tweets dataset is affected slightly because in Twitter, people tend not to use modifiers and numerals in time expressions.

5.4.6 Computational Efficiency

We briefly discuss the computational efficiency of TOMN in comparison with the five state-of-the-art baselines. HeidelTime, SUTime, SynTime, ClearTK, and TOMN are implemented by the Java language, while UWTime is implemented by Python. For the rule-based methods, HeidelTime and SUTime run nearly in real time, and SynTime runs in real time. Table 5.7 presents the running time that TOMN and the learning-based baselines cost to complete a whole process (including both training and test) on the three datasets on a Mac OS laptop (1.4GHz Processor and

Table 5.7 Running time that TOMN and the two learning-based baselines cost to complete a whole process, including both training and test (unit: seconds)

Method	TE-3	WikiWars	Tweets
ClearTK	152	223	86
UWTime	864	1050	160
TOMN	36	48	42

8GB Memory). In practice, UWTime implements both time expression recognition and normalization, while ClearTK and TOMN implement only the time expression recognition. Different programming languages and different concerning tasks might be factors that affect the computational efficiency, however, from Table 5.7 we still can see that TOMN is more efficient than ClearTK and UWTime. Considering only the test, TOMN runs in real time.

5.5 Discussion

The analysis of time expressions can explain many empirical observations that are reported in other works about time expression recognition. For example, UzZaman et al. report that using an extra large-scale of dataset does not improve the performance of time expression recognition [21]; Bethard reports that using the TimeBank dataset alone performs better than using the TimeBank and AQUAINT datasets together on time expression recognition [1]; Filannino et al. report that features of gazetteers, shallow parsing, and propositional noun phrases do not contribute a significant improvement on time expression recognition [6]. These observations can be explained by the characteristics illustrated in Sect. 3.1.2. Characteristics 2, 3, 4, and 5 together suggest that additional gazetteers, large corpus, and more datasets provide no further useful information but repeated time tokens and their loose combinations, and that those syntactic features cannot provide extra useful information for a CRFs-based learning method to model time expressions.

The analysis of tagging schemes can explain many empirical observations that are reported in other works about the impact of the BIO (or IOB2) and BILOU (or IOBES) schemes in named entity recognition and classification (NERC). Ratinov and Roth report that the BILOU scheme outperforms the BIO scheme on the MUC-7 and CoNLL03 NERC datasets [14]; Dai et al. report that the IOBES scheme performs better than the IOB2 scheme in drug name recognition [5]. When looking at their results, however, we find that those improvements are rather slight, most of them are less than 1%; in some cases, the BIO scheme performs better than the BILOU scheme. Lample et al. confirm that they do not observe the significant improvement of the IOBES scheme over the IOB2 scheme on the CoNLL03 NERC dataset [9]. These observations can be explained by our analysis of tagging schemes in Sects. 5.1 and 5.4.5. Basically, the BIO and BILOU schemes are based on *the positions within labeled chunks* and implicitly assume that target entities should be formed by a fixed structure and even fixed collocations. But entities as part of language are actually flexible. When applied to entity recognition, the BIO and BILOU schemes would more or less suffer from the problem of *inconsistent tag assignment*. We analyze the named entities in the CoNLL03 (English NERC) dataset [15] as an example. We find that for each of the CoNLL03's training, development, and test sets, more than 53.7% of distinct words appear in different positions within named entities; more than 93.7% of named entities each has at least one word not appearing in common text; the named entities on average contain 1.45 words, with 63.2% one-word named entities. The percentage 53.7% is similar to the one of distinct time tokens in time expressions, which is 53.5% (see Characteristic 5); the percentage 93.7% is similar to the one of time expressions that contain time tokens, which is 91.8% (see Characteristic 2); the length distribution is similar to the one of time expressions in the Tweets dataset (see Characteristic 1). That means named entities demonstrate some common characteristics similar to time expressions. When modeling named entities, like modeling time expressions, the BIO and BILOU schemes would either suffer from the problem of inconsistent tag assignment or be roughly equivalent if they are approximately reduced to the constituent-based BO and UO schemes. In either case, the difference between the two schemes impacts slightly.

When analyzing the CoNLL03 dataset (which contains four entity categories: PER, LOC, ORG, and MISC), we find that some named entities are annotated with different entity categories. In its training set, for example, "Wimbledon" is annotated 4 times with LOC, 8 times with ORG, and 18 times with MISC. Such named entities (including several polysemy) in the training set, development set, and test set reach relatively high percentage of respective 6.9%, 4.4%, and 6.5%. The inconsistent annotation and inconsistent tag assignment may be able to explain why most state-of-the-art NERC systems achieve the F_1 at around 94.5% on the development set and around 91.5% on the test set [4, 9, 11–14, 22], and why more than 10 years' effort improves the F_1 by only 0.8% on the development set (from 2003s 93.9% [7] to current 94.7% [12]) and by only 2.9% on the test set (from 2003s 88.7% [7] to current 91.6% [4]). The two inconsistency problems seem to limit the upper bound of the performance on development set at near 94.5% and the one on test set at near 91.5%. This suggests that to further improve the performance on the current CoNLL03 dataset with current methods is difficult and unreliable. Instead of continuing to fine-tune current methods, we should try to correct the inconsistent annotation and address the problem of inconsistent tag assignment.

References

1. Bethard S (2013) Cleartk-timeml: a minimalist approach to tempeval 2013. In: Proceedings of the 7th international workshop on semantic evaluation, p 10–14
2. Chang AX, Manning CD (2012) Sutime: a library for recognizing and normalizing time expressions. In: Proceedings of 8th international conference on language resources and evaluation, pp 3735–3740
3. Chang AX, Manning CD (2013) Sutime: evaluation in TempEval-3. In: Proceedings of the second joint conference on lexical and computational semantics (SEM), p 78–82
4. Chiu JP, Nichols E (2016) Named entity recognition with bidirectional LSTM-CNNs. Trans Assoc Comput Linguist 4:357–370
5. Dai HJ, Lai PT, Chang YC, Tsai RTH (2015) Enhancing of chemical compound and drug name recognition using representative tag scheme and fine-grained tokenization. J Cheminform 7.S1(S14):1–10
6. Filannino M, Brown G, Nenadic G (2013) Mantime: temporal expression identification and normalization in the TempEval-3 challenge. In: Proceedings of the 7th international workshop on semantic evaluation, p 53–57

7. Florian R, Ittycheriah A, Jing H, Zhang T (2003) Named entity recognition through classifier combination. In: Proceedings of the 7th conference on natural language learning, p 168–171

8. Lafferty J, McCallum A, Pereira F (2001) Conditional random fields: probabilistic models for segmenting and labeling sequence data. In: Proceedings of the 18th international conference on machine learning, p 281–289

9. Lample G, Ballesteros M, Subramanian S, Kawakami K, Dyer C (2016) Neural architecture for named entity recognition. In: Proceedings of the 15th annual conference of the North American chapter of the association for computational linguistics, p 260–270

10. Lee K, Artzi Y, Dodge J, Zettlemoyer L (2014) Context-dependent semantic parsing for time expressions. In: Proceedings of the 52th annual meeting of the association for computational linguistics, p 1437–1447

11. Luo G, Huang X, Lin CY, Nie Z (2015) Joint named entity recognition and disambiguation. In: Proceedings of the 2005 conference on empirical methods in natural language processing, p 879–888

12. Ma X, Hovy E (2016) End-to-end sequence labeling via bi-directional LSTM-CNNs-CRF. In: Proceedings of the 54th annual meeting of the association for computational linguistics (vol 1: long papers), p 1064–1074

13. Passos A, Kumar V, McCallum A (2014) Lexicon infused phrase embeddings for named entity resolution. In: Proceedings of the 8th conference on computational language learning, p 78–86

14. Ratinov L, Roth D (2009) Design challenges and misconceptions in named entity recognition. In: Proceedings of the thirteenth conference on computational natural language learning, p 147–155

15. Sang EFTK, Meulder FD (2003) Introduction to the CoNLL-2003 shared task: language-independent named entity recognition. In: Proceedings of the 7th conference on natural language learning, p 142–147

16. Sang EFTK, Veenstra J (1999) Representing text chunks. In: Proceedings of the ninth conference on european chapter of the association for computational linguistics, p 173–179

17. Stevens SS (1946) On the theory of scales of measurement. Science 103(2684):677–680

18. Strötgen J, Gertz M (2010) Heideltime: high quality rule-based extraction and normalization of temporal expressions. In: Proceedings of the 5th international workshop on semantic evaluation (SemEval'10). Association for Computational Linguistics, Stroudsburg, p 321–324

19. Strötgen J, Zell J, Gertz M (2013) Heideltime: tuning English and developing Spanish resources. In: Proceedings of the second joint conference on lexical and computational semantics (SEM), p 15–19

20. Strötgen J, Bogel T, Zell J, Armiti A, Canh TV, Gertz M (2014) Extending heideltime for temporal expressions referring to historic dates. In: Proceedings of the 9th international conference on language resources and evaluation, p 2390–2397

21. UzZaman N, Llorens H, Derczynski L, Verhagen M, Allen J, Pustejovsky J (2013) Semeval-2013 task 1: TempEval-3: Evaluating time expressions, events, and temporal relations. In: Proceedings of the 7th international workshop on semantic evaluation, p 1–9

22. Xu M, Jiang H, Watcharawittayakul S (2017) A local detection approach for named entity recognition and mention detection. In: Proceedings of the 55th annual meeting of the association for computational linguistics, p 1237–1247

23. Zhong X (2020) Time expression and named entity analysis and recognition. PhD thesis, Nanyang Technological University, Singapore

24. Zhong X, Cambria E (2018) Time expression recognition using a constituent-based tagging scheme. In: Proceedings of the 2018 world wide web conference, Lyon, France, p 983–992

25. Zhong X, Sun A, Cambria E (2017) Time expression analysis and recognition using syntactic token types and general heuristic rules. In: Proceedings of the 55th annual meeting of the association for computational linguistics, Vancouver, vol 1, p 420–429

Chapter 6
UGTO: Uncommon Words and Proper Nouns

Abstract The conventional position-based tagging schemes that previous research used to model named entities suffer from the problem of inconsistent tag assignment. To overcome the problem of inconsistent tag assignment, we define a constituent-based tagging scheme termed UGTO scheme to model named entities under conditional random fields with uncommon words and proper nouns as features. In addition, many researchers jointly model multiple linguistic tasks with an implicit assumption that these individual tasks can enhance each other via the joint modeling. Before conducting research on jointly modeling multiple tasks, however, such researchers hardly examine whether such assumption is true or not. In this chapter, we empirically examine whether named entity classification improves the performance of named entity recognition as an empirical case of examining whether semantics improves the performance of a syntactic task. Evaluation shows that named entity recognition does not lie at the semantic level and is not a semantic task, instead, it is a syntactic task, and that the joint modeling of named entity recognition and classification does not improve the performance of named entity recognition. Evaluation also demonstrate that traditional hand-crafted-feature models can achieve state-of-the-art performance in comparison with the auto-learned-feature model on named entity recognition.

Keywords Named entities · Constituent-based tagging scheme · Uncommon words · Proper nouns · Syntactic task · Semantic task

In this chapter, we firstly describe our proposed model UGTO that is used to recognize named entities from unstructured text, and then, we give the way of empirically examining whether a linguistic task is a syntactic task or a semantic task. After that, we design four experiments to compare our proposed model UGTO with two representative state-of-the-art models and examine whether named entity classification improves the performance of named entity recognition [24, 26, 27].

6.1 UGTO: Uncommon Words and Proper Nouns

Characteristics 6 and 7 suggest that for a dataset, those words of its development set and test set that hardly appear in the common text of its training set tend to predict named entities, and those words are mainly proper nouns. This is our main idea for named entity recognition. Figure 6.1 visualizes this idea with a simple example: in the unannotated test set, those words like "Boston" and "Reuters" that hardly appear in the common text of the annotated training set tend to predict named entities. Such words are also called *uncommon words* and they include two kinds: the first kind of uncommon words appears in the named entities of the training set (e.g., "Boston" and "Africans") while the second kind does not (e.g., "Reuters"). The remaining of this chapter illustrates how we develop our idea in UGTO.

UGTO models named entities under a CRFs framework and follows a typical CRFs procedure. Figure 6.2 shows the overview of UGTO in practice. It mainly includes four components: (1) uncommon word induction, (2) word lexicon, (3) UGTO scheme, and (4) named entity modeling, with the help of uncommon words, word lexicon, and the UGTO scheme.

6.1.1 Uncommon Word Induction

For each dataset, we induce two kinds of uncommon words from the *annotated training set* and the *unannotated test set*.

The first kind of uncommon words is induced from the annotated training set. At first, there is an empty list L. For each word w in the named entities of the training set, we calculate its rate ($r(w)$) of hardly appearing in the common text of the training set by Eq. (3.4). If $r(w)$ reaches a threshold R, then we add w to L. Like the setting in Sect. 3.2.2, R is set to 1 for the CoNLL03 dataset and to 0.95 for the OntoNotes* dataset.

The second kind of uncommon words is induced from the unannotated test set. They include those words (excluding those in L) that appear in the unannotated test set and do not appear in the common text of the training set. Inducing them is to recognize out-of-vocabulary named entities. This kind of uncommon words can be viewed as the information derived from unannotated data, and note that they can be only used in the test phase, because the unannotated test set is not available in the training phase.

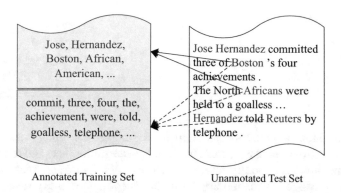

Annotated Training Set   Unannotated Test Set

Fig. 6.1 Main idea: those words (red font) of unannotated test set that hardly appear in the annotated the common text of the training set (bottom-left) are likely to predict named entities. Such words include two kinds: the first kind (e.g., "Boston") appears in the annotated named entities of the training set (top-left) while the second kind (e.g., "Reuters") does not. The training set is highlighted by colored background that means annotated. The test set instead is unannotated. Solid arrow denotes appearing in the named entities of the training set while dashed arrow denotes hardly appearing in the common text of the training set

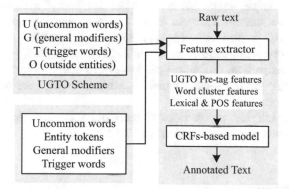

Fig. 6.2 Overview of UGTO in practice. The top-left side shows the UGTO scheme that consists of four tags. The bottom-left side are the uncommon words and word lexicon. The right-hand side shows named entity modeling, with the help of the UGTO scheme and uncommon words and word lexicon

6.1.2 Word Lexicon

Word lexicon includes two kinds of entity-related words: entity tokens and modifiers. Entity tokens are collected from external sources: some entity tokens are from the entity list provided by the CoNLL03 shared task [23] and some are from

Table 6.1 Statistics of word lexicon

Word lexicon	Number
Entity token	9658
Generic modifier	17
PER trigger word	31
Other trigger word	116

Wikipedia.[1] Modifiers are collected from the training set according to the annotation guideline of the dataset; they include two kinds: generic modifiers and trigger words. Generic modifiers can modify several categories of entity tokens, such as "of" and "and," while trigger words modify a specific categories of entity tokens, such as "Mr." modifying PER entity tokens and "Inc" modifying ORG entity tokens.

For these entity tokens, we put all of them together, without using their entity categories (e.g., PER, LOC, and ORG), so as to remove the impact of semantic information carried in their entity categories. For the trigger words, we separate PER trigger words from other trigger words because PER trigger words appear outside named entities while other trigger words appear inside named entities.

Unlike previous works that use lexicon in word sequences [9, 22], we use lexicon in words. For example, we do not use "Boston University" but use "Boston" and "University." This strategy leads our model to a high coverage and more efficient. For example, with n distinct words, our model can identify up to n one-word sequences, n^2 two-word sequences, n^3 three-word sequences, etc. Furthermore, during feature extraction, our model needs only to scan the text word by word, avoiding the difficulty of choosing which algorithm for sequence matching and its computational cost.

Table 6.1 summarizes the statistics of the word lexicon. Note that these word lexicon is collected with only a little effort.

6.1.3   UGTO Scheme

Characteristic 8 states that named entities are formed by loose structure and suggests to explore another appropriate tagging scheme. We then design another constituent-based tagging scheme termed UGTO scheme to encode uncommon words and word lexicon for named entity modeling. The UGTO scheme consists of four tags: U, G, T, and O; they indicate and encode the constituent words of named entities. Specifically, U encodes uncommon words and entity tokens. G encodes generic modifiers while T encodes trigger words. O encodes those words outside named entities.

---

[1]https://en.wikipedia.org/wiki/Lists_of_cities_by_country   and   https://en.wikipedia.org/wiki/Lists_of_people_by_nationality.

6.1.4 Named Entity Modeling

Similar to time expression modeling, named entity modeling also includes two parts: (1) feature extraction and (2) model learning and sequence tagging.

6.1.4.1 Feature Extraction

The features we extract for named entity modeling include three kinds: UGTO pre-tag features, word cluster features, and basic lexical and POS features. During feature extraction, the i-th word in text is denoted by w_i.

UGTO Pre-tag Features The UGTO pre-tag features are designed to encode the information of uncommon words and word lexicon under our UGTO scheme. Specifically, a word is encoded by U if it satisfies two conditions: (1) it appears in the list L induced in Sect. 6.1.1 (i.e., the first kind of uncommon words) or does not appear in the common text of the training set (i.e., the second kind of uncommon words[2]); (2) it has a POS tag of NNP* or is matched by an entity token or is hyphenized by at least one entity token (e.g., "U.S.-based" and "English-oriented"). A word is encoded by G if it is matched by any of the generic modifiers. A word is encoded by TP if it is matched by any of the PER trigger words. A word is encoded by T if it is matched by other trigger words.

Besides the UGTO pre-tag features, we use two features to indicate (1) whether a word is matched by any of entity tokens and (2) whether a word is hyphenized by any of entity tokens.

Word Cluster Features Previous works have demonstrated that word clusters are useful for many information extraction tasks [11, 15]. We follow these works to derive the prefix paths of 4, 8, and 12 bits from a set of hierarchical word clusters as features for a word. In practice, we use the publicly available word clusters "bllip-clusters"[3] for the CoNLL03 dataset and use the one[4] trained by the OntoNotes 5.0 corpus [21] for the OntoNotes* dataset.

Lexical and POS Features The lexical and POS features are widely used for named entity modeling and we extract three kinds of such features for w_i: (1) the word w_i itself, its lowercase, and its lemma; (2) whether its first letter is capitalized and whether it is the beginning of a sentence; (3) its POS tag.

Feature Values Similar to the setting of feature values for TOMN described in Sect. 5.3.1, the UGTO pre-tag features and word cluster features are treated as

---

[2]Note that this kind of uncommon words is not available in the training phase because they are induced from the unannotated test set.

[3]http://people.csail.mit.edu/maestro/papers/bllip-clusters.gz.

[4]https://drive.google.com/file/d/0B2ke42d0kYFfN1ZSVExLNlYwX1E/view.

Table 6.2 Extracted features for the word w_i for named entity modeling

1	UGTO pre-tag features in a 5-word window of w_i, namely pre-tags of w_{i-2}, w_{i-1}, w_i, w_{i+1}, and w_{i+2}
2	Whether w_i is matched by any entity token; whether w_i is hyphenized by any entity token
3	Prefix paths of 4, 8, and 12 bits from a set of hierarchical word clusters for w_i
4	w_i itself, its lowercase, its lemma, whether the first letter is capitalized, where it is the beginning of a sentence, its POS tag

separate features with binary values, while the basic lexical and POS features are incorporated with multiple values under a features.

Table 6.2 summarizes the features extracted for w_i for named entity modeling. For the UGTO pre-tag features and lexical and POS features, we extract them in a 5-word window of w_i, namely the features of w_{i-2}, w_{i-1}, w_i, w_{i+1}, and w_{i+2}. For the word cluster features, we consider them for only the current w_i.

6.1.4.2   Model Learning and Sequence Tagging

UGTO models named entities with the above extracted features under a CRFs framework. Similar to TOMN described in Chap. 5, in experiments, UGTO uses Stanford Tagger[5] to obtain the information of word lemma and POS tags and uses a Java version of CRFSuite[6] with its default parameters as the CRFs framework for model learning and sequence tagging. Note that the UGTO scheme is used in two different phases with two different functional uses: (1) during feature extraction, it is used as pre-tags to encode uncommon words and word lexicon; (2) during model learning and sequence tagging, it is used as labeling tags.

After model learning and sequence tagging, we extract named entities from these tagged sequences. For those models that exclude entity categories from labeling tags, the U, G, and T words (i.e., non-O words) that appear together form a named entity (see Fig. 6.3a–c). For those models that incorporate entity categories into labeling tags, the consecutive non-O words that are tagged with the same entity category together form a named entity (see Fig. 6.3d–f).

6.2   Syntactic Task and Semantic Task

In this section, we describe how to empirically determine whether a linguistic task is a syntactic task or a semantic task, according to Chomsky's syntactic theory [1, 2] and Katz and Fodor's foundation of semantic theory [3, 8, 16, 17].

---

[5]http://nlp.stanford.edu/software/tagger.shtml.
[6]http://www.chokkan.org/software/crfsuite/.

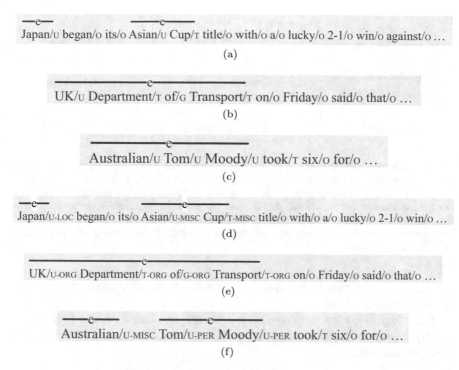

Fig. 6.3 Examples of named entities extracted from tagged sequences. The label *e* indicates named entities. The first three examples (i.e., **a–c**) demonstrate the extraction in the models that exclude entity categories from labeling tags during model learning and sequence tagging, while the last three (i.e., **d–e**) demonstrate the extraction in the models that incorporate entity categories into labeling tags. (**a**) Consecutive non-O words together form a named entity. (**b**) Consecutive non-O words together form a named entity. (**c**) Consecutive non-O words together form a named entity. (**d**) Consecutive words that are tagged with the same entity type form a named entity. (**e**) Consecutive words that are tagged with the same entity type form a named entity. (**f**) Consecutive words that are tagged with the same entity type form a named entity

On the one hand, Chomsky's syntactic theory suggests that syntax does not appeal to semantics; in other words, semantics does not affect the study of syntax [1, 2]. On the other hand, semantic theory treats syntactic structures (i.e., grammar) as a part of it, but it requires the syntactic analysis to be completed before starting semantic analysis [3, 8, 16, 17]. According to both the syntactic theory and semantic theory, we outline the relationships between syntax and semantics and between syntactic tasks and semantic tasks in Fig. 6.4, with referring to the Figure 6 and Figure 7 in [8]. It contains three levels in the layout of syntactic-semantic structure: lexical level, syntactic level, and semantic level. In the lexical level, there are specific tokens, phrases, and sentences, which are general units or components we see in languages. The syntactic level lies at the middle and stores syntactic information that is employed for syntactic structures (i.e., grammar) construction and other syntactic tasks. Above the syntactic level is the semantic level where

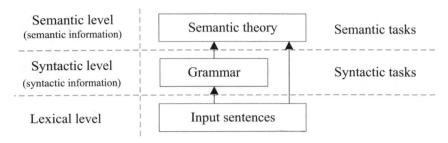

Fig. 6.4 Relations between syntactic theory and semantic theory (the middle part) and between syntactic tasks and semantic tasks (the right-hand side), with referring to the syntactic theory by Chomsky [1, 2] and the one of semantic theory by Katz and Fodor [8]. The lexical level lies at the bottom and includes specific tokens, phrases, and sentences; in the middle is the syntactic level that stores syntactic information for grammar construction and other syntactic tasks; the semantic level lies above the syntactic level where semantic information is for semantic theory development and other semantic tasks

semantic information is stored and is employed for semantic theory development and other semantic tasks.

According to the layout of syntactic-semantic structure shown in Fig. 6.4, we specify the way to empirically determine whether a linguistic task is a syntactic task or a semantic task.

Semantic Task To verify that a linguistic task is a semantic task, we need only to verify that semantic information is more effective than syntactic information for this task; or empirically speaking, using semantic information achieves higher performance than using syntactic information on this task. Because the semantic level lies above the syntactic level, if the semantic information is more effective for a linguistic task than the syntactic information, then the linguistic task must be a semantic task.

Syntactic Task To verify that a linguistic task is a syntactic task, we need to conduct experiments that satisfy the following two conditions: (1) using lexical and syntactic information can achieve state-of-the art performance for this linguistic task and (2) adding or using semantic information can not improve the performance on this task. The first condition indicates that this task is at least a syntactic task, and the second condition indicates that this task is not a semantic task. If a linguistic task is at least a syntactic task but not a semantic task, then it must be a syntactic task.

We would like to emphasize that the relationships between syntax and semantics and between syntactic tasks and semantic tasks belong to linguistic phenomena, and they are independent of those statistical models that we employ to process the language text. That means these phenomena will appear in most state-of-the-art models. Therefore, if a linguistic phenomenon is empirically demonstrated to appear in a state-of-the-art model, then theoretically speaking, this linguistic phenomenon will also appear in other state-of-the-art models.

6.3 Evaluation

6.3.1 Setup

Datasets The two benchmark datasets we use for the experiments of named entity recognition are CoNLL03 [23] and OntoNotes* [21]. They are detailed in Sect. 3.2.1.

Compared Methods The compared methods include two representative state-of-the-art methods: StanfordNERC [4] and LSTM-CRF [10]. StanfordNERC derives hand-crafted features under CRFs with the BIO scheme. LSTM-CRF derives automatic features learned by long short-term memory networks (LSTMs) [6] under CRFs with the IOBES scheme. We use StanfordNERC as the representative of those traditional hand-crafted-feature methods and LSTM-CRF as the representative of those auto-learned-feature methods.

Evaluation Metrics We use the evaluation toolkit of the CoNLL03 shared task [23] to report results under the three standard metrics: *Precision* (*Pr.*), *Recall* (*Re.*), and F_1.

These three evaluation metrics are similar to the ones defined by Eqs. (4.1), (4.2), and (4.3), respectively, except the meanings of TP, FP, and FN. In named entity recognition, TP (true-positive) denotes the number of named entities that are recognized by the model and simultaneously appear the ground-truth, FP (false-positive) denotes the number of named entities that are recognized by the model but do not appear in the ground-truth, while FN (false-negative) denotes the number of named entities appearing in the ground-truth but are not recognized by the model.

6.3.2 Experimental Design

We design the following four experiments to evaluate UGTO against the two representative baselines with two goals. The first goal is to examine whether the joint NERC task can improve the NER performance, and this goal is denoted by *G1*. The second goal is to examine whether semantic information can improve the NER performance, and this goal is denoted by *G2*.

- **Experiment 1** *Do not incorporate entity types into labeling tags in the whole process, including modeling, tagging, and evaluation.*

- **Experiment 2** *Incorporate entity types into labeling tags during modeling and tagging (i.e., training and testing), but not the evaluation.*

- **Experiment 3** *Add word embeddings as features to the model in Experiment 1.*

- **Experiment 4** *Add word embeddings as features to the model in Experiment 2.*

To easily explain the goals of these designed experiments, we let $< \mathbf{X}, Y >$ be the representations for words, where $\mathbf{X}$ denotes the feature vectors and Y denotes the labeling tags.

Experiment 1 is a basic and pure task of named entity recognition, in which a model excludes entity categories from labeling tags in the whole process. Designing this experiment is to test the quality of UGTO against the two baselines and to learn syntactic information from context without learning semantic information.[7] The labeling tags of UGTO include {U, G, T, O}; the ones of StanfordNERC include {B, I, O}; the ones of LSTM-CRF include {I, O, B, E, S}.

Experiment 2 is a joint talk of named entity recognition and classification, in which a model incorporates entity categories into labeling tags during modeling and tagging. Designing this experiment is to answer the question: *whether does named entity classification enhance named entity recognition during modeling?* In this experiment, the labeling tags of a model include the combinations of basic tags and entity categories. Specifically, the labeling tags of UGTO on the CoNLL03 dataset include thirteen tags { U-PER, U-LOC, U-ORG, U-MISC, G-PER, G-LOC, G-ORG, G-MISC, T-PER, T-LOC, T-ORG, T-MISC, O }. Similarly, the labeling tags for StanfordNERC and LSTM-CRF on the CoNLL03 dataset include the combinations of their basic tags and entity categories, such as B-PER, B-LOC, B-ORG, B-MISC, I-PER, I-LOC, I-ORG, I-MISC, and O.

Designing Experiment 3 is to achieve the goal *G2* by incorporate semantic information into features $\mathbf{X}$. Word embeddings are proposed to capture both the syntactic and semantic information from large corpus [7, 13, 20]. The Figure 3 in [20] suggests that word embeddings capture much more semantic information than syntactic information from context. Therefore, adding word embeddings into a model can incorporate semantic information into features $\mathbf{X}$ for modeling, and thus can examine whether semantic information can improve the NER performance.

Designing Experiment 4 is to achieve both the goals *G1* and *G2* by conducting Experiment 2 and Experiment 3 simultaneously, namely merging Experiments 2 and 3 into an experiment.

In all the above four experiments, we report only the NER performance of UGTO and the two baseline models. Specifically, after recognizing named entities from unstructured text, we convert tagged text to the CoNLL-format with the BIO scheme for evaluation; the BIO scheme indicates the **B**eginning word, the **I**nside word in a named entity, and those words appearing **O**utside named entities. For Experiments 2 and 4, we remove entity types during evaluation; more specifically, we incorporate entity types into labeling tags during modeling and tagging, but remove entity types during evaluation, so that we can evaluate the impact of the joint NERC task on

---

[7]Language context contains both the syntactic and semantic information, and statistical models (e.g., word embeddings [7, 13, 20]) can learn both the information from context. A model that is optimized for NER does not aim to learn the semantic information but aims to learn the syntactic from context, while a model that is optimized for NEC aims to learn the semantic information from context. In this paper, we are mainly concerns with the impact of the semantic information that is learned from context for the NER performance.

the NER performance. We do the same conversion and evaluation for all the three models, namely UGTO, StanfordNERC, and LSTM-CRF.

6.3.3   Experimental Results

Table 6.3 reports the overall NER performance of UGTO and the two baselines conducted in the four experiments described above on the two datasets. Note again that we are mainly concerned with the NER performance and Table 6.3 and 6.5 report only the performance on named entity recognition, without named entity classification. For the LSTM-CRF model, as mentioned above, since it already leverages auto-learned features and takes into account embedding features, we do not conduct Experiments 3 and 4 for it.

Table 6.3 Named entity recognition performance of UGTO and baselines conducted on the CoNLL03 and OntoNotes* datasets in the four experiments. The subscript "$E1$" represents Experiment 1; "$E2$" represents Experiment 2; "$E3$" represents Experiment 3; and "$E4$" represents Experiment 4. [a]Indicates that the improvement of our result over the best one of baselines is statistically significant ($p < 0.05$ under t-test)

Dataset	Method	Development set			Test set		
		$Pr.$	$Re.$	F_1	$Pr.$	$Re.$	F_1
CoNLL03	StanfordNERC$_{E1}$	95.80	95.93	95.86	93.28	93.59	93.43
	StanfordNERC$_{E2}$	**96.43**	95.36	95.89	93.77	92.49	93.13
	StanfordNERC$_{E3}$	95.97	95.82	95.89	93.34	93.46	93.40
	StanfordNERC$_{E4}$	95.78	95.49	95.63	93.64	93.12	93.38
	LSTM-CRF$_{E1}$	94.96	95.46	95.21	92.02	93.48	92.74
	LSTM-CRF$_{E2}$	95.68	94.36	95.02	92.99	91.55	92.27
	UGTO$_{E1}$	95.84	**96.21**	**96.02**	94.15[a]	**94.56**[a]	**94.35**[a]
	UGTO$_{E2}$	96.24	95.76	96.00	**94.29**[a]	94.18[a]	94.23[a]
	UGTO$_{E3}$	95.74	95.79	95.77	93.04	93.66	93.35
	UGTO$_{E4}$	96.07	95.52	95.80	93.85	92.67	93.26
OntoNotes*	StanfordNERC$_{E1}$	92.38	91.62	92.00	93.11	91.99	92.54
	StanfordNERC$_{E2}$	**93.17**	91.17	92.16	**93.69**	90.96	92.31
	StanfordNERC$_{E3}$	92.45	91.48	91.96	92.98	91.92	92.45
	StanfordNERC$_{E4}$	93.09	91.16	92.11	93.21	90.88	92.03
	LSTM-CRF$_{E1}$	91.41	91.86	91.64	92.35	91.91	92.13
	LSTM-CRF$_{E2}$	92.52	90.32	91.41	93.37	90.28	91.80
	UGTO$_{E1}$	93.28	**92.08**[a]	**92.67**[a]	93.43	**92.26**	92.84[a]
	UGTO$_{E2}$	93.32	92.01[a]	92.66[a]	93.62	92.17[a]	**92.89**[a]
	UGTO$_{E3}$	92.06	91.66	91.86	93.38	91.41	92.38
	UGTO$_{E4}$	92.27	91.35	91.81	93.45	91.22	92.32

In the following few subsections, we analyze these experimental results and demonstrate the empirical examination of our goals *G1* and *G2* described in Sect. 6.3.2.

6.3.3.1   Experiment 1

Table 6.3 shows that UGTO$_{E1}$ achieves either the best results or near the best results among all the three models; the differences between UGTO$_{E1}$ and the best results in all the F_1 are less than 0.27%, which ranges within the scope of experimental errors. Note that in Experiment 1, the model does not aim to learn semantic information from context, and that UGTO$_{E1}$ derives only lexical and syntactic features [26]. That means, using only lexical and syntactic features achieves state-of-the-art performance on the single NER task, and this indicates that the NER task is at least a syntactic task.

Table 6.3 also shows that StanfordNERC$_{E1}$ performs comparably with UGTO$_{E1}$ and LSTM-CRF$_{E1}$ performs worse than UGTO$_{E1}$. Note again that UGTO$_{E1}$ derives only the lexical and syntactic features. By contrast, both the StanfordNERC and LSTM-CRF models are originally designed for the joint NERC task, with an aim to learn semantic information from context for the NEC task. The experimental results however demonstrate that those semantic information learned by StanfordNERC$_{E1}$ and LSTM-CRF$_{E1}$ does not improve the NER performance. This indicates that the NER task does not lie at the semantic level and is not a semantic task.

6.3.3.2   UGTO$_{E2}$, UGTO$_{E3}$, UGTO$_{E4}$ vs. UGTO$_{E1}$

We add three public word embeddings into UGTO, and they are (1) word2vec, which is trained on the Google News dataset [13], (2) GloVe, which is trained on the Wikipedia 2014 and Gigaword 5 corpora [20], and (3) FastText, which is trained on the Wikipedia 2017, UMBC corpus, statmt.org news, and Common Crawl datasets [7, 14]. We try all the embeddings of word2vec (300-dimension), GloVe (50-, 100-, 200-, and 300-dimension), and FastText (300-dimension) and the GloVe 50-dimension version achieves the best results with the least runtime, therefore we report the results of using GloVe 50-dimension embeddings to analyze the impact of word embeddings features on the NER task.

From Table 6.3 we can see that UGTO$_{E2}$, UGTO$_{E3}$, and UGTO$_{E4}$ perform either comparably with or worse than UGTO$_{E1}$ on both datasets. The differences of their performance range from 0.23% to 0.86%, which is within the scope of experimental errors. That means, both the semantic information that are incorporated from entity types into labeling tags and incorporated from word embeddings into features do not further improve the NER performance but simply cost additional runtime.[8] This indicates again that the NER task does not lie at the semantic level and is not a semantic task.

6.3.3.3 StanfordNERC vs. LSTM-CRF

Table 6.3 shows that the StanfordNERC performs either comparably with or slightly better than the LSTM-CRF in the NER task. According to the literature, however, LSTM-CRF significantly outperforms StanfordNERC in the joint NERC task on the CoNLL03 dataset; specifically, LSTM-CRF achieves the result of F_1 at 90.94% on the test set of the CoNLL03 dataset [10] while StanfordNERC achieves the result of F_1 at only 86.86% [4]. That means those features that are learned by the LSTM-CRF model for the NEC task do not improve the NER performance. Since the NEC task is a semantic task, those features learned by LSTM-CRF for the NEC task mainly includes semantic information; however, those learned semantic information is not effective for the NER task. This therefore indicates again that the NER task does not lie at the semantic level and is not a semantic task.

6.3.3.4 Experiment 2 vs. Experiment 1

For each model, we compare its performance in Experiment 2 with its performance in Experiment 1 so as to analyze the impact of entity types on the NER performance. Table 6.3 shows that on both datasets, $UGTO_{E2}$ and $UGTO_{E1}$ achieve similar performance on the NER task; $StanfordNERC_{E2}$ and $StanfordNERC_{E1}$ achieve similar performance on the NER task; and $LSTM-CRF_{E2}$ and $LSTM-CRF_{E1}$ also achieve similar performance on the NER task. That means the semantic information that is incorporated into labeling tags from entity types does not improve the NER performance. This further indicates that the NER task does not lie at the semantic level and is not a semantic task.

To conclude, the above extensive experimental results demonstrate that the NER task is a syntactic task but not a semantic one, and that the joint NERC task does not improve the NER performance.

---

[8]The syntactic information from word embeddings does not improve the NER performance, because $UGTO_{E1}$ already leverages sufficient lexical and syntactic information (which includes those syntactic information learned from context) that covers the syntactic information from word embeddings.

Table 6.4 Controlled experiments using UGTO on the CoNLL03 and OntoNotes* datasets for analyzing the impact of syntactic information on the NER performance. Subscript "$E5$" represents Experiment 5; "$E6$" represents Experiment 6; and "$E7$" represents Experiment 7

Dataset	Method	Dev. set			Test set		
		$Pr.$	$Re.$	F_1	$Pr.$	$Re.$	F_1
CoNLL03	UGTO$_{E1}$	**95.49**	**95.81**	**95.65**	**93.81**	**94.44**	**94.12**
	UGTO$_{E5}$	94.62	95.29	94.95	91.87	93.41	92.63
	UGTO$_{E6}$	82.63	71.88	76.88	73.70	60.48	66.44
	UGTO$_{E7}$	94.64	95.05	94.84	91.66	92.60	92.13
OntoNotes*	UGTO$_{E1}$	**92.32**	**92.08**	**92.20**	**93.43**	**91.67**	**92.55**
	UGTO$_{E5}$	91.60	91.44	91.52	92.91	91.54	92.22
	UGTO$_{E6}$	80.75	66.50	72.93	82.52	67.81	74.44
	UGTO$_{E7}$	91.41	91.06	91.23	92.80	91.34	92.06

6.3.4   Syntactic Information for the NER Task

Besides the four experiments described in Sect. 6.3.2, we also conduct three more controlled experiments using the UGTO model to analyze the impact of syntactic information on the NER task. These three controlled experiments are designed as Experiment 5, 6, and 7, and they demonstrate that (1) syntactic information is effective for the NER task, (2) word embeddings contain some syntactic information that is useful for the NER task, and (3) those syntactic information from word embeddings does not further improve the NER performance.

• **Experiment 5** *Remove the syntactic features from UGTO in Experiment 1, which mainly include the part-of-speech (POS) tags especially the NNP/NNPS tags.*

• **Experiment 6** *Use only the GloVe 50-dimension word embeddings for the NER task in Experiment 1. That is, use only the word embeddings as features under the CRFs framework with the UGTO scheme.*

• **Experiment 7** *Add word embeddings as features to UGTO in Experiment 5.*

The results of these three experiments are reported in Table 6.4, in which the subscript "$E5$" represents Experiment 5, "$E6$" represents Experiment 6, and "$E7$" represents Experiment 7. Note that in these three experiments, we do not incorporate entity types into labeling tags. For convenient comparison and discussion, Table 6.4 also reports the results of UGTO$_{E1}$ that is directly copied from Table 6.3.

6.3.4.1   UGTO$_{E5}$ vs. UGTO$_{E1}$

Table 6.4 shows that the performance of UGTO$_{E5}$ decreases in certain extent in comparison with the one of UGTO$_{E1}$. This means that after syntactic features are removed from the UGTO model, its performance is hurt, and this indicates that the syntactic features are effective for the NER task. But we can see that such decrease is not very significant, with only absolute 0.33–1.49% in the F_1. The reason is that statistical models like CRFs can learn syntactic information from context; and those syntactic information that is learned from context for the POS tagging can also be learned from context for the NER task. That means the syntactic information either learned directly from context or carried by the POS tags is effective for the NER task.[9]

Our explanation is also supported by those empirical observations which are reported in other works. On the one hand, the Stanford NLP group reports that the StanfordNERC tagger derives similar features as StanfordPOS tagger does and the performance of their tagger benefits little from the POS tags (see the description under Question 16 at https://nlp.stanford.edu/software/crf-faq.html). That means those information that is learned for the POS tagging is similar to the those that is learned for the joint NERC task, and it is effective for both the POS tagging and the joint NERC task. Note that POS tags are syntactic types and POS tagging is a syntactic task, therefore those information that is learned for the POS tagging is syntactic information. On the other hand, entity types are semantic types and the research working on the NEC task reports that semantic information is much more effective than syntactic information for the NEC task [5, 12, 18], which demonstrates that the NEC task is a semantic task. And since those information that is effective for POS tagging is syntactic information and it is effective for the NERC task but not effective for the NEC task, those syntactic information must be effective for the NER task.

6.3.4.2   UGTO$_{E6}$ vs. UGTO$_{E1}$

Table 6.4 suggests that although word embeddings carry certain amount of syntactic information that is effective for the NER task, such quantity is far less than the one that is learned from context by UGTO$_{E1}$. This performance is consistent with the observation that is reported by Pennington et al. [20]: word embeddings capture only a few syntactic information which is far less than those semantic information that is captured by the same word embeddings model (see Fig. 6.3 in their paper).

6.3.4.3   UGTO$_{E7}$ vs. UGTO$_{E5}$

Table 6.4 shows that UGTO$_{E7}$ does not perform better than UGTO$_{E5}$. That means the syntactic information carried by word embeddings does not further improve the performance of a state-of-the-art model on the NER task. This is consistent with the observation reported in Sect. 6.3.3. The reason, as illustrated above, is that a state-of-the-art model can learn much more syntactic information from context than those

---

[9]In fact, the syntactic information that is carried by the POS tags is also learned from context.

syntactic information that is carried by word embeddings. Of cause, as demonstrated before, the semantic information that is carried by word embeddings is effective for the NEC task but not effective for the NER task.)

To conclude for this subsection, our extensive experiments and thorough analysis demonstrate that syntactic information significantly influences the NER performance. This indicates that the NER task is a syntactic task. Together all the results of all the seven experiments described in both Sects. 6.3.2 and 6.3.4, we demonstrate clearly that the NER task is a syntactic task, and is not a semantic task.

6.3.5   Factor Analysis in Experiment 1

We conduct controlled experiments to analyze the impact of UGTO labeling tags and those features that are used in UGTO. The experimental results for factor analysis are reported in Table 6.5.

Impact of UGTO Labeling Tags To analyze the impact of the UGTO labeling tags, we replace them by the BIO tags (as well as the IOBES tags) and keep other factors unchanged. The BIO and IOBES schemes achieve similar results and we report the results of the BIO scheme as a representative. $UGTO_{E1}$ performs better than BIO, because the BIO and BILOU schemes suffer from the problem of inconsistent tag assignment, while the UGTO scheme overcomes this problem [25].

Impact of UGTO Pre-tag Features We remove the UGTO pre-tag features from $UGTO_{E1}$ so as to analyze their impact. We can see that the UGTO pre-tag features significantly improve the performance, with about absolute 2.0% improvements.

Impact of Word Cluster Features Word cluster features are helpful in UGTO (about 0.45% improvement) but are not significant as their impact in some other works [11, 15, 19, 22]. The reason is that the UGTO pre-tag features play a

Table 6.5 Impact of factors. "BIO" indicates the systems that replace UGTO labeling tags by BIO tags. "$-$" indicates removing this factor from $UGTO_{E1}$

Dataset	Method	Development set			Test set		
		$Pr.$	$Re.$	F_1	$Pr.$	$Re.$	F_1
CoNLL03	$UGTO_{E1}$	**95.84**	**96.21**	**96.02**	**94.15**	**94.56**	**94.35**
	BIO	94.78	95.14	94.96	93.66	94.02	93.83
	$-$UGTO PreTag	94.68	93.23	93.95	93.47	91.04	92.34
	$-$Word Clusters	95.09	94.96	95.02	94.01	93.23	93.62
OntoNotes*	$UGTO_{E1}$	**93.28**	**92.08**	**92.67**	**93.43**	**92.26**	**92.84**
	BIO	92.63	91.05	91.83	92.87	91.35	92.10
	$-$UGTO PreTag	92.65	90.08	91.35	92.71	89.64	91.15
	$-$Word Clusters	92.67	90.74	91.69	93.22	92.16	92.68

similar role as word clusters in improving the coverage and connecting words at an abstraction level.

6.4 Limitations

There is a limitation in UGTO: when extracting named entities from tagged sequence, UGTO would wrongly treat several consecutive entities as a named entity. Comparing the two examples in Fig. 6.3c, f, for example, UGTO wrongly extracts the two named entities "Australian" and "Tom Moody" as a named entity "Australian Tom Moody."

For the examination on whether semantics aids syntax, although our analysis and experiments demonstrate that neither the NEC task alone nor the joint NERC task can further improve the NER performance, there are still some potential limitations in our work that require to be resolved in the future. One limitation is that our analysis on the NER and NEC tasks is just an empirical case of examining whether semantics or semantic information can improve the performance of a syntactic task. To fully examine the proposition of whether semantics can aid syntax, we still need to examine many other syntactic tasks such as syntactic parsing to see whether semantics or semantic information could improve those syntactic tasks. In the future, we will continue such kinds of examinations to justify the validity or invalidity of this proposition. Another limitation is that although our experiment are designed to learn syntactic information or semantic information from context, we could not guarantee that those models learn only the syntactic information without learning any semantic information, nor that those models learn only the semantic information without learning any syntactic information. What is even worse, it is still not clear whether we could separate syntactic information from semantic information. In the future, we will also try to resolve these issues.

References

1. Chomsky N (1957) Syntactic structures. Mouton Publishers, Berlin
2. Chomsky N (1965) Aspects of the theory of syntax. MIT Press, Cambridge
3. Dowty DR, Wall RE, Peters S (1981) Introduction to montague semantics. Reidel, Dordrecht
4. Finkel JR, Grenager T, Manning C (2005) Incorporating non-local information into information extraction systems by Gibbs sampling. In: Proceedings of the 43nd annual meeting of the association for computational linguistics, p 363–370
5. Giuliano C (2009) Fine-grained classification of named entities exploiting latent semantic kernels. In: CoNLL
6. Hochreiter S, Schmidhuber J (1997) Long short-term memory. Neural Comput 9:1735–1780
7. Joulin A, Grave E, Bojanowski P, Mikolov T (2017) Bag of tricks for efficient text classification. In: Proceedings of the 15th conference of the European chapter of the association for computational linguistics, p 427–431
8. Katz JJ, Fodor JA (1963) The structure of a semantic theory. Language 39(2):170–210

9. Kazama J, Torisawa K (2007) Exploiting Wikipedia as external knowledge for named entity recognition. In: Proceedings of the 2007 joint conference on empirical methods in natural language processing and computational natural language learning, p 698–707
10. Lample G, Ballesteros M, Subramanian S, Kawakami K, Dyer C (2016) Neural architecture for named entity recognition. In: Proceedings of the 15th annual conference of the North American chapter of the association for computational linguistics, p 260–270
11. Liang P (2005) Semi-supervised learning for natural language. Master's thesis, Massachusetts Institute of Technology
12. Ling X, Weld DS (2012) Fine-grained entity recognition. In: Proceedings of the twenty-sixth conference on artificial intelligence
13. Mikolov T, Sutskever I, Chen K, Corrado G, Dean J (2013) Distributed representations of words and phrases and their compositionality. In: Proceedings of 27th conference on neural information processing systems, pp 3111–3119
14. Mikolov T, Grave E, Bojanowski P, Puhrsch C, Joulin A (2018) Advances in pre-training distributed word representations. In: Proceedings of the international conference on language resources and evaluation
15. Miller S, Guinness J, Zamanian A (2004) Name tagging with word clusters and discriminative training. In: Proceedings of the human language technology conference of the North American chapter of the association for computational linguistics
16. Montague R (1970) Universal grammar. Theoria 36:373–398
17. Montague R (1973) The proper treatment of quantification in ordinary English. In: Approaches to natural language, p 221–242
18. Nakashole N, Tylenda T, Weikum G (2013) Fine-grained semantic typing of emerging entities. In: Proceedings of the 51st annual meeting of the association for computational linguistics, p 1488–1497
19. Owoputi O, O'Connor B, Dyer C, Gimpel K, Schneider N, Smith NA (2013) Improved part-of-speech tagging for online conversational text with word clusters. In: Proceedings of NAACL-HLT 2013, p 380–390
20. Pennington J, Socher R, Manning C (2014) Glove: global vectors for word representation. In: Proceedings of the 2014 conference on empirical methods in natural language processing, p 1532–1543
21. Pradhan S, Moschitti A, Xue N, Ng HT, Bjorkelund A, Uryupina O, Zhang Y, Zhong Z (2013) Towards robust linguistic analysis using ontonotes. In: Proceedings of the 7th conference on computational natural language learning, p 143–152
22. Ratinov L, Roth D (2009) Design challenges and misconceptions in named entity recognition. In: Proceedings of the thirteenth conference on computational natural language learning, p 147–155
23. Sang EFTK, Meulder FD (2003) Introduction to the CoNLL-2003 shared task: language-independent named entity recognition. In: Proceedings of the 7th conference on natural language learning, p 142–147
24. Zhong X (2020) Time expression and named entity analysis and recognition. PhD thesis, Nanyang Technological University, Singapore
25. Zhong X, Cambria E (2018) Time expression recognition using a constituent-based tagging scheme. In: Proceedings of the 2018 world wide web conference, lyon, France, p 983–992
26. Zhong X, Cambria E, Hussain A (2020) Extracting time expressions and named entities with constituent-based tagging schemes. Cogn Comput 12(4):844–862
27. Zhong X, Cambria E, Hussain A (2021) Does semantics aid syntax? An empirical study on named entity recognition and classification. Neural Comput Appl

Chapter 7
Conclusion and Future Work

Abstract In this book, we present our works on the analysis and recognition of time expressions and named entities. We summarize five intrinsic characteristics about time expressions and three ones about named entities. According to these characteristics, we propose three methods to recognize time expressions and named entities from unstructured text, namely SynTime, TOMN, and UGTO. When analyzing named entities, we find that the joint task of named entity recognition and classification cannot improve the performance of the subtask of named entity recognition.

Keywords Time expressions · Named entities · Intrinsic characteristics

We conduct an in-depth analysis on four diverse datasets for the intrinsic characteristics of time expressions and summarize five such common characteristics [1–3]. The first four characteristics provide evidence in terms of time expressions for Zipf's principle of least effort [6] and the last one demonstrate the flexibility of time expressions. According to these characteristics, we propose two methods to recognize time expressions from unstructured text, including a type-based method termed SynTime and a learning-based method termed TOMN. SynTime is inspired by the part-of-speech of language and defines a syntactic token type system for the constituent words of time expressions, and designs a small set of general heuristic rules to recognize time expressions based on the idea of boundary expansion. Since these heuristic rules are only relevant to token types and are independent of specific tokens, SynTime is independent of specific domains, specific text types and even specific languages that consists of specific tokens. TOMN is a CRFs-based learning method with a defined constituent-based tagging scheme to model time expressions. The constituent-based tagging scheme overcomes the problem of inconsistent tag assignment that is caused by the conventional position-based tagging schemes. Experimental results on three diverse datasets demonstrate the effectiveness, efficiency, and robustness of SynTime and TOMN compared with state-of-the-art baselines, including rule-based time taggers and learning-based time taggers. Moreover, our analyses of time expressions and tagging schemes help explain many empirical results and observations that are reported in previous works about time expression recognition and tagging schemes in named entity recognition.

Similar to our analysis on time expressions, we also analyze two benchmark datasets for the intrinsic characteristics of named entities and summarize such three common characteristics [4]. These three characteristics motivate us to design a learning-based method termed UGTO to model named entities, with another defined constituent-based tagging scheme and only a kind pre-tag features, word cluster features, and some basic lexical and POS features. Experiments on two benchmark datasets demonstrate the effectiveness of UGTO against two representative state-of-the-art methods. Experimental results also demonstrate that joint modeling of named entity recognition and classification does not improve the performance of named entity recognition, in both our model and the two representative models.

When analyzing named entities, we find that our evaluation has justified that named entity recognition is a syntactic task while named entity classification is a semantic one, and that the joint modeling of named entity recognition and classification cannot improve the performance of named entity recognition [5]. However, to empirically justify whether semantics aids syntax in a joint modeling framework, we still need to conduct more experiments involved other linguistic tasks. In the future work, we will conduct those experiments to empirically examine such question: does semantics aid syntax under a joint modeling framework?

In addition, we will also conduct research on time expression normalization so as to complete the end-to-end task of time expression recognition and normalization and develop useful software for public use.

References

1. Zhong X (2020) Time expression and named entity analysis and recognition. PhD thesis, Nanyang Technological University, Singapore
2. Zhong X, Cambria E (2018) Time expression recognition using a constituent-based tagging scheme. In: Proceedings of the 2018 world wide web conference, Lyon, France, p 983–992
3. Zhong X, Sun A, Cambria E (2017) Time expression analysis and recognition using syntactic token types and general heuristic rules. In: Proceedings of the 55th annual meeting of the association for computational linguistics, Vancouver, vol 1, p 420–429
4. Zhong X, Cambria E, Hussain A (2020) Extracting time expressions and named entities with constituent-based tagging schemes. Cogn Comput 12(4):844–862
5. Zhong X, Cambria E, Hussain A (2021) Does semantics aid syntax? An empirical study on named entity recognition and classification. Neural Comput Appl
6. Zipf G (1949) Human behavior and the principle of least effort: an introduction to human ecology. Addison-Wesley, Readings

Printed in the United States
by Baker & Taylor Publisher Services